Foreword by the Chairman

The Royal Commission on Criminal Procedure was appointed in February 1978. Its terms of reference require it to study and make recommendations on the process of the pre-trial criminal procedure in England and Wales. Essentially it has had to do four things: first, to examine the powers and duties of the police in the investigation of crime and the way that these affect the rights of the suspect; second, to study the existing system for prosecuting criminal offences; third, in doing this, to bear in mind the national need to use resources efficiently and economically; and lastly, to give regard to the proper balance between the interests of the community in seeking to bring offenders to justice and in protecting the rights and liberties of persons suspected or accused of crime.

This is the second volume containing studies on police interrogation which have been undertaken on behalf of the Royal Commission. Research Study Number 3 is a survey of some of the sociological, legal and, to a lesser extent, psychological writings on police interrogation. It was undertaken by the late Pauline Morris in the latter part of 1977 in order to provide the Royal Commission at the start of its work with a comprehensive picture of the information about and arguments surrounding police interrogation. Dr. Morris' survey has since been somewhat overtaken by events, not least by the empirical studies carried out on the Commission's behalf. One of these, by Paul Softley and his colleagues at the Home Office Research Unit, forms the second part of this volume. The study is based on observations of police interviews conducted at four police stations. It describes the operation of the Judges' Rules and Administrative Directions to the Police and assesses the contribution of questioning to the detection of crime. An enlarged version of this report is being published as a Home Office Research Study.

On behalf of the Royal commission I wish to offer our thanks to all those who assisted with these studies. The views expressed in the reports are, of course, those of the authors and not of the Royal Commission.

Cyril Philips

Cyril Philips
April 1980

Contents

Police Interrogation:
Review of Literature

Pauline Morris

Contents

CHAPTER 1

Introduction

The aims of this report are:

a. to give an account of the nature of police interrogation – what is known about the conduct of the police and of suspects and accused during interrogation.
b. to try to assess the effect of interrogation in general – or of particular features of the procedures that govern it – upon the criminal process as a whole.
c. to develop any other material which bears more or less directly upon the subject, for example the psychological aspects of interrrogation.

The focus is, as far as possible, on the specific question of interrogation but it is crucial to stress that pre-trial interrogation cannot usefully be considered in isolation, and without reference to trial and post-trial procedures. As Baldwin and McConville (1977) point out: 'The importance of the defendant's encounter with the police can scarcely be over-stated for, in the great majority of cases, what takes place at that stage can critically influence what happens at later stages of the criminal process' (p.105).[1] Matters such as the rules of evidence, plea (or bail) bargaining and sentencing will undoubtedly affect, and be affected by, the nature of the interrogation process.

Furthermore, there are important definitional issues of a legal nature which *precede* the interrogation and which need to be considered, insofar as they affect subsequent procedures; for example, the confusion which surrounds such concepts as 'arrest', 'detention' and 'custody' (LaFave, 1965; Lanham, 1974; Lidstone, 1977; Zander, 1977a, 1977b). Finally, there is the vast (and vexed) question of police discretion and cautioning (Steer, 1970; Goldstein, 1963; Wilcox, 1972).[2] In this report no attempt has been made to deal with these issues in any depth; they will be referred to only insofar as they directly affect the discussion of interrogation.

---

[1] See also Bottoms and McClean (1976) p 230
[2] The references given here, as elsewhere in the text, are essentially samples taken from a vast literature on the particular topic. Limitations of time prevented a more comprehensive survey.

Preparation and scope of the report

The principal sources consulted in the preparation of this report were the writings of lawyers, policemen, social scientists and psychologists and psychiatrists. However, in the course of undertaking the work, I had the opportunity to meet a considerable number of people with practical knowledge of police work either as members (or ex-members) of the force, as researchers, or as administrators. Where appropriate, I have used these discussions to inform my understanding of the literature and, even more important, to expand it, since there is a noticeable dearth of empirical material concerning the actual practice of interrogation, particularly in this country. It would seem that in England a number of research workers have been permitted to sit in at interrogations (usually as part of a wider study of policing) but they have not necessarily been in a position to publish their observations. Furthermore, such findings as have been published are primarily of interest by virtue of the theoretical issues that they raise; from a scientific viewpoint, much of the material lacks methodological rigour.[1] This point needs to be stressed not only because it places severe limitations on the validity of discussing interrogation *practice,* but also because it contrasts markedly with the more open attitude to police research in North America.[2]

Most of the literature surveyed here relates to England and Wales and the United States, though an attempt has been made to broaden the discussion by reference to Australia and Canada. As has been pointed out many times, comparisons between United States and Commonwealth practices in respect of criminal investigation must be viewed in the light of differing legal frameworks and social environments. Glasbeek and Prentice (1968) have drawn particular attention to the fact that the Bill of Rights as an integral part of the United States Constitution has no counterpart in the Commonwealth,[3] nor are the rights of the accused in the Commonwealth countries generally regulated by a comprehensive body of legislation. They further argue that an increasing crime rate, the findings of the Wickersham Committee on Law Enforcement,[4] and the majority findings in *Miranda*[5] have all led American courts 'to play an

---

[1] Glanville Williams (1960) states: 'No study has been made of their [the practice of detention and questioning] precise extent. We do not know how many persons in any one year are taken to the police station for questioning; how often the legal requirements of a valid arrest are satisfied; how long suspects are detained without charge; how much questioning takes place late at night; how many are released without charge. We do not know the conditions of the questioning or what blandishments, threats or trickery may sometimes be used' (p.328). A thorough search of the literature indicates little change since these words were written, although an important exception is to be found in Chatterton, (1976a).

[2] See, for example, Wald *et al* (1967) and Reiss (1971).

[3] The Bill of Rights in Canada is regarded by the authors to be 'merely declaratory in effect'.

[4] National Commission on law Observance and Enforcement, *Report of Lawlessness in Law Enforcement,* 1931.

[5] *Miranda v Arizona* 384 US 436 (1966) established the right of persons in custody to be told a. of their right to remain silent; b. that anything they say can be used against them in subsequent criminal proceedings; c. of their right to counsel during interrogation and d. that if they cannot afford an attorney, one will be provided at state expense. These are known as the *Miranda* warnings.

activist role in the control of the police' which is not reflected in the Commonwealth countries where there is 'no equivalent feeling of urgency and the courts have been correspondingly more passive'. Finally, these authors argue that the police in the Commonwealth countries are held in higher esteem by both the judiciary and the public. Having drawn attention to these factors, Glasbeek and Prentice nevertheless go on to suggest that the central problem is the same in the United States and in the Commonwealth countries, namely determining the degree to which the accused should be made a witting or unwitting instrument in his own condemnation. Specifically, the issue is to what extent the police may exploit 'the timidity, ignorance, lack of foresight, and stupidity of the suspect in order to obtain a conviction' (p.474). If this is indeed the central problem surrounding criminal investigation in general, and interrogation in particular, then it is as much a philosophical issue as a legal one, and if it is to be considered in that light, there is no reason to exclude from consideration the literature and practices of foreign jurisdictions.

The literature on interrogation falls neatly into four categories – legal arguments, police views, sociological perspectives and a very much smaller number of psychological writings. It is, I think, significant that within these four groups there is very little overlap (though a vast amount of repetition!). The authors write from very different perspectives which reflect the basic assumptions of their professional backgrounds. It would seem that they only rarely study the writings of those from other disciplines (footnotes, where used, tend to reflect the incestuous nature of their perspectives) and where reference *is* made to the writings of those from other disciplines, this is usually a mere passing acknowledgement rather than a means of opening up the discourse. Since the bulk of the literature on interrogation is of a legal nature, this report aims to provide a sociological flavour. Legal provisions and legal arguments are therefore dealt with at only a very superficial level, a situation that may not mattter unduly since it seems that most legal writing is based on theory rather than practice, the 'ought' rather than the 'is'.

Finally, whilst there is inevitably a high degree of overlap between the various sections of the report, I have tried to deal firstly with the general social context of crime investigation and of interrogation in particular, then to move on to a discussion of the interrogating process, looking at both theory and practice (insofar as material is available on the latter) and finally to review some of the proposals for future developments and to raise some of the more philosophical and sociological questions which remain unanswered.

CHAPTER 2

The social context of interrogation

Law enforcement and the police

For the policeman on the job there are few clear guidelines concerning his law enforcement role. While policies and procedures emanating from the highest level certainly play an important part in the discretionary power he is expected to exercise, so do divisional policies and procedures, tradition and pressures by peers. These various sources often present conflicting or competing demands and as a result, officers will tend to resolve any tensions arising out of the situation by performing their tasks in ways which maximise rewards and minimise strains for the organisations and the individuals involved (Chambliss and Seidman, 1971, p.266). In this way it is the police who shape 'law-in-action' (i.e. the implementation of the law) by virtue of their ability to control enforcement practices.[1,2]

These views are supported by empirical research in both this country and the United States: 'One of the most extensively documented facts about police work is that the police under-enforce certain laws and jealously protect the discretion which that implies' (Chatterton 1976a, p.113). Amongst other things, Chatterton researched how police officers in England decide to invoke the law relating to public order on some occasions and not on others. He argues that a useful starting point is to 'look at the charges themselves, suspending the conventional idea that laws are things to be enforced and thinking of them instead as resources to be used to achieve the ends of those who are entitled or able to use them. If we do not explore the meanings which

---

[1] A simple example recounted to me many times during the course of preparing this report concerns the very considerable number of cases which reach detectives every day and which they are expected to 'solve'. Time does not allow for more than a few to be dealt with, so apart from really serious cases, the selection tends to be based upon the question 'will there be a body at the end?'. In other words, cases that look unpromising from a clear-up point of view are less likely to be handled.

[2] In developing their argument, Chambliss and Seidman of course go much further than this and show how the contradictory demands for 'law and order' combine with the bureaucratic organisation of police work to further the adoption of a 'crime control' rather than a 'due process' model of police procedure. They illustrate this by reference to police discrimination against non-whites and poor whites who have less power to complain. The development of this argument seems of considerable relevance to any consideration of the criminal process, but falls outside the terms of reference of this report.

policemen build into the framework of charges supplied in legislation we run into the danger of making inferences from the law as it is written in the books which may have little, if any, relevance to the way control processes operate in practice' (p.114).

Chatterton's research findings lead him to suggest that the vagueness of legislation governing public order is an advantage to the practical policeman in his peace-keeping role. He found that operational ranks shared certain routine understandings about several public order charges – that it was expected (correctly as it turned out) that the majority of persons charged with certain offences would plead guilty in any case.

Chatterton goes on to relate the invoking of charges to certain aspects of police occupational culture. He found that police officers were concerned to protect a number of interests in their peace-keeping work. Most notably, they were anxious to avoid 'trouble', both with their supervising officers and with the public, for example, by using arrest as a threat, to be invoked only when other alternatives failed. This is not the place to give details of Chatterton's findings: the point to stress is his finding that lower-ranking officers had very varying styles of approach to their work which need to be understood by higher-ranking officers and by those 'experts' from outside who recommend changes about police work. 'The decisions which policemen make are made in a context of low visibility, and their organisational superiors could be said to sustain this by adopting a policy of "let sleeping dogs lie" and using the absence of a complaint . . . as the criterion of effectiveness' (p.121).

The above remarks relate specifically to the initial encounter between policemen and suspects, but the main concern of police officers – to avoid or minimize trouble – would seem to apply equally to subsequent police action, including the decision to question, and the process of interrogation.

In the United States, Bittner (1974) also draws attention to the fact that in police work there exists little more than 'inchoate law' and that what gets done depends on the individual perspicacity, judiciousness and initiative of the police officer. Reiss and Bordua (1966) attempt to show how police discretion and disparity stem in good part from the general organisation of modern police work. The relationships that the police have with various categories of citizen lead to variations in the degree to which formal legality is extended to the different categories. This is difficult to control, given that policing is itself highly decentralised and involves numbers of officers working alone, and out of range of direct supervision. Other Americans write in similar vein: Skolnick (1966) argues that the police officer is confronted with conflicting demands by his organisation – on the one hand productivity (high clearance rates) and on the other hand adherence to a set of formal procedures which impede productivity. Since productivity is a matter of record (and a source of promotion), officers tend to resolve their dilemma in its favour.

This view is shared by Pogrebin (1976) who points out that for a detective the most important measure of his efficiency has come to be the clearance rate; this opinion is also held by Tifft (1975) and by Wilson (1977). Pogrebin suggests that the clearance rate has important implications not only for the way that police officers carry out their work in relation to producing suspects, but also in respect of their relationship with colleagues. Thus clearance rates may be heavily dependent upon informants and this in turn may lead to a lack of cooperation between detectives, each one being anxious to retain the services of particular informants. Reciprocal trade-offs between investigators and informants make it dangerous to share information.[1] Skolnick (1966) puts it succinctly. 'Where means are found to raise production (higher clearance rates) rules are circumvented not with impunity, however, but only under the strain of production quotas' (p.180).

Finally, it should be noted that in both the United States and the United Kingdom the policeman's conduct may be greatly affected by his position within a particular police agency – division, rank and setting all affect the work and the perspectives of policemen (see in particular Westley, 1970; Cain, 1971; and Reiss, 1971). Most such studies have been concerned primarily with uniformed policemen, though Pogrebin's (1976) work relates specifically to the detective role.

All the factors mentioned above are as important in their effect upon the interrogation process as upon any other aspect of police work. If consideration is to be given to the need for changes in the rules and regulations relating to interrogation, these wider issues will be crucial, since the behaviour of police officers is affected by these organisational and attitudinal factors as much as, if not more than, by any formal rules that may be laid down. The point is well summed up by Chatterton (1976a): 'lack of knowledge has not prevented people from speculating about the subject [police work] or from making recommendations about how police work should be improved, even though these proposals are so vague and general that policemen, if they *were* motivated to change their behaviour, would find little guidance about what they should do to meet the abstract ideals propounded by these "experts". Consequently, unsupported inferences about the policing process have passed imperceptibly into our conception of police work, and proposals for change have taken the form of general statements about what the police ought to be doing which are often superficial glosses on a complex problem . . . [reasonably minded police officers] . . . are both angered by the way that their decisions and actions are misrepresented and frustrated by calls for improvement which are too far removed from the practical context of the situations they face to provide any positive help or guidance.' (p.120).

Public expectations of the police role

Relatively little appears to have been written about public expectations of the police role; according to the President's Commission on Law Enforcement and the Administration of Justice (1967), '. . . there is a widespread popular conception of the police, supported by the news and entertainment media. Through these, the police have come to be viewed as a body of men continually engaged in the exciting, dangerous, and competitive enterprise of apprehending and prosecuting criminals. Emphasis upon this one aspect of police

---

[1] In the United Kingdom possibly the most obvious example in modern times of the dangers of such procedures concerns recent enquiries into the Metropolitan Police. See Cox *et al* (1977).

functioning has led to a tendency on the part of both the public and the police to underestimate the range and complexity of the total police task' (p.13).

A report on policing in Ontario[1] also indicates that crime solving and law enforcement were popularly referred to as the main components of the police role. On the one hand the public expects criminal activity to be prevented and suppressed in order to preserve an orderly society, on the other hand democratic tradition places a high priority on individual liberty and freedom of action. It is when a policeman who pursues the former principle comes into contact with an individual who pursues the latter that there is the greatest possibility of conflict (Royal Commission into Metropolitan Toronto Police Practices, 1976).

In this country, Lambert (1970) draws attention to a general trend in policing away from ideals which value good community relations and towards 'legalistic' alternatives which emphasise criminal law enforcement and the maintenance of public order. One unfortunate aspect of such a change is to be found in deteriorating relations between police and minority groups — specifically black people. Also in this country Cain (1973), and in the United States, Rubenstein (1973) suggest from their empirical research that there is little or no evidence of the kind of policing that values good community relations in preference to law enforcement and public order definitions of the police task.

The reason for raising the issue in this report is, however, not a desire to find out *more* about public expectations, rather it is to suggest that it is the general public who decide what level of law enforcement they want from the police. Chatterton (1976b) draws attention to this specifically in relation to offences against the person. But others have suggested that it is also true for many other types of offence (Reiss and Bordua, 1967; Reiss, 1971; Bottomley and Coleman, 1976). They point out that self-initiated police intervention is relatively rare, and that most police work is *reactive,* that is to say the police wait for information from the public before acting. Most researchers agree with Reiss (1971) who writes that 'most knowledge that contributes to a solution through investigation is based on citizen information on the identity of the suspects'.

Criminal investigation and the 'need' for interrogation

In manuals and text books about methods of criminal investigation[2] (almost all of which are American) it is noteworthy that many authors tend to use the terms 'questioning', 'interrogating' and 'interviewing' as though they were synonymous. On the other hand, some go to great lengths to define these various terms very precisely (though they may revert to using them interchangeably!); thus, for example, Van Meter (1973) distinguishes between

---

[1] The Task Force on Policing in Ontario, *Report to the Solicitor General,* 1974.
[2] All the books mentioned here (and many in similar vein) are to be found on the shelves at Bramshill Police College, though the extent to which they are read is unclear. Deeley (1971) argues, and this was confirmed by many people to whom I spoke, that in England techniques of interrogation are picked up on the job, as distinct from the American experience where instruction manuals are used much more generally.

'interviewing' which is designed to obtain further information, and 'interrogation' which is designed to obtain a confession. Wicks (1974) defines interviewing as being to secure data and 'interrogation' as being *either* to get an admission of guilt, *or* to obtain clarification and elaboration of certain facts from someone who is innocent.

The most comprehensive yet the most complex description of the situation is given by Mettler (1977) who distinguishes between an 'interview' which he describes as a 'verbal communication between the police officer and another person . . . to ascertain the truth of a situation by obtaining and testing answers to pertinent questions *re* an alleged or suspected violation of the law', and 'interrogation' which he defines as 'the questioning of a suspect or a reluctant witness, the nature of which is more adversarial than that used in a non-adversarial interview . . . The investigator's skill must be of a higher order. The primary object of an interrogation is not . . . to obtain a confession . . . it is rather to obtain information. Information thus gained may be classified as a confession (an acknowledgement of guilt), an admission (an incriminating statement that indicates but falls short of acknowledged guilt), or a statement (a declaration of facts concerning the case under investigation or even concerning extraneous matters).'

These varying definitions of what I shall subsume under a general heading of 'interrogation', may be of more than semantic importance to those who write about them, but for the policeman − or more specifically the detective − charged with clearing up criminal cases, there seems, from the literature, to be little doubt that 'the basic purpose of an interrogation is to attempt to secure a confession' (Milte and Weber, 1977, p.117).

Despite this, Deeley (1971) claims that policemen have neither the time nor the inclination to interrogate every suspect and he quotes one British chief constable who claimed that policemen are very reluctant to interrogate except where it is absolutely necessary and that a proper interrogation was carried out in only one case in fifteen (p.138).

'Necessity' as interpreted by the police, seems to be related to the existence or otherwise of other evidence. It is upon this point that there is considerable disagreement. There are those who say that one should not interrogate unless one has sufficient evidence to justify such action; there are others (and impressionistically these would seem to be the majority) who say that they have insufficient time to obtain other evidence, and interrogation is a necessary first step which will then enable them to go out and obtain confirmation of what they have learned and thus collect other evidence. Deeley reports the head of an English provincial force who estimated that confessions resulted from seven out of ten interrogations. 'Once you have your confession then you go on from facts revealed to build up your evidence. But it was interrogation, and that alone, which broke the case' (pp.139−140).

A related, yet more general question is one to which Weisberg (1961) draws attention, namely the fact that secret questioning in a police station has come to be thought of as necessary to effective law enforcement.[1] He illustrates this

---

[1] He also points out that one would be hard put to explain to visitors from a legal Mars how such secret questioning fits into a system of criminal law which recognises the privilege against self-incrimination and the right to counsel.

by reference to Inbau – one of the most active proponents of such a position – (1961), to Bator and Vorenberg (1966), and to Williams (1961). Their arguments appear to be based upon the view that a stable and safe society is dependent upon an efficient police department and therefore sacrifices of individual rights must be made in order to achieve this end. Witt (1973) notes that 'intertwined with this rationale is the assumption that men with honest motives and purposes do not remain silent when their honour is assailed'.

There have been two major pieces of empirical research (both American) which have, *inter alia,* attempted to ascertain the *police's evaluation of the importance of interrogation,* and to determine the *need for interrogation.*[1] In both studies, detectives were asked whether there were other ways in which investigation could possibly replace interrogation as a means of crime solution. Sixty five per cent of the 43 detectives interviewed by Witt replied with an absolute 'no', a figure that compares with 71 per cent of the 21 officers interviewed in the New Haven Study. In the Witt study, 7 per cent of detectives thought interrogation could be eliminated without loss to law enforcement; the comparable figure in New Haven was 10 per cent. In order to determine whether interrogation was essential *in practice* to the solution of crime, Witt examined 478 police files. Interrogation was found to be essential or important in 24 per cent of the cases and unimportant or unnecessary in 76 per cent of them. Comparable figures in the new Haven Study were 13 per cent and 86 per cent.[2] Witt concludes that 'in most cases interrogation was not needed to solve the immediate crimes of which the suspects were accused'.

Witt recognises that interrogation may serve a number of functions other than that of obtaining a confession to the crime under investigation. Twelve per cent of interrogations led to the implication of accomplices, 10 per cent led to the recovery of stolen property, in 15 per cent of interrogations suspects cleared themselves and 18 per cent led to the solution of other crimes. Although there is no comparable information in this country, the extent to which detection rates are dependent on suspects admitting offences which are then taken into consideration is worthy of note. Lambert (1970), for example, found that as many as 44 per cent of a sample of detected property crimes were cleared as a result of being taken into consideration while Bottomley and Coleman (1976) found one third of detected indictable offences were cleared in this way. Commenting on clear-up rates as a measure of police efficiency, Lambert notes: 'It is surely curious that the only measure of police efficiency and one that is widely publicised, is very dependent upon the whim of offenders declaring their interest in previous exploits in the probably groundless hope that they will receive better treatment in court. This dependence on getting offenders to confess to maintain a success rate has, I believe, important consequences for police administration and organisation' (p.43).

It is widely held by police officers that clear-up rates are an important avenue to promotion. They will therefore continue to press suspects for confessions, not only to the offence under investigation, but to other offences

---

[1] Wald *et al* (1967), referred to below as the New Haven Study, and Witt (1973).
[2] Readers interested in the reasons for these differences should refer to the footnotes in the article by Witt.

which they may or may not have committed. Since some offenders hope that this will result in kinder treatment in court, such admissions may be seen as of mutual advantage to both parties.

Confession as a basis of a conviction

'Even if evidence is strong, its treatment in court by the defence makes a signed confession invaluable to the prosecution' (Lewis, 1976). Not only does a confession help convince the jury, it also 'simplifies proceedings and avoids the attendance of witnesses who may be inconvenienced, embarrassed, or even threatened by the accused's associates' (Franklin 1970, p.93).

Lord Devlin (1960) writes: '. . . the accused's statement to the police officer plays a great part in the prosecution's case. There can be no doubt of that and I should emphasise it. In any study of the inquiry into crime it would be far less important than it is to examine police methods of interrogation if it were not true to say that the evidence which such interrogation produces is often decisive. The high degree of proof which the English legal system requires – proof beyond reasonable doubt – often could not be achieved by the prosecution without the assistance of the accused's own statement' (p.48).

Laurie (1970), basing his views on data collected by Martin and Wilson (1969), expresses the view that 'every contested case involves a detective in an average of two weeks' extra work'. This is because it involves finding and persuading witnesses, taking two sets of statements, report writing, the completion of numerous forms, dealing with recovered property, and appearing in court on a number of occasions to ask for a remand. Laurie comments: 'every plea of not guilty is a threat to the detective's precariously balanced work load'.

In a study by McCabe and Purves (1972a) the authors report: 'While there were occasional, sometimes glaring, exceptions to this rule, it was generally correct to say that the acquittal of a defendant was attributable to a single cause – the failure of the prosecution (normally the police) to provide enough information, or to present it in court in a way that would convince both judge and jury of the defendant's guilt' (p.11). In a subsequent study these researchers (1972b) comment: 'To secure a conviction the prosecution must hurdle without fail all the obstacles placed before it in the discharge of its heavy burden of proof, and must do it to the satisfaction of the jury – a jury which seems often to be as critical of the prosecution performance as it is credulous of the defendant's explanations for his activities' (p.20). In the United States, Weisberg (1961) refers to what he calls 'a subtle corruption of the jury traceable to interrogation practices'. He argues that so long as the search for confessions remains so important in police work, and so many prosecutions rely on them, juries may come to feel that a charge unsupported by a confession is weaker than it really is (p.35).

Discussions with lawyers and police officers in this country indicate widespread agreement concerning the advantages of a confession, and certainly there is some support for this view in the United States (see, for example, Kuh, 1966). However, the opposite view emerges from empirical studies carried out in the United States dealing with the relationship between interrogation and confession; these conclude that the value of confessions has been grossly exaggerated, and several authors agree that most cases can be solved by other investigative techniques.[1]

Apart from the studies by McCabe and Purves (where the question was touched upon but was not central to the research) no one in this country appears to have examined the truth of the statement that it is difficult to obtain a conviction based on evidence unsupported by a confession. If it is indeed true, then it would be important to know in what ways it is problematical. By focusing solely on confessions, almost all existing studies (and they are mainly American) have neglected to examine cases where evidence is available, but no confession; nor have there been satisfactory studies which consider whether other methods of investigation would have produced sufficient conclusive evidence, without reliance on confessions. It would therefore seem important to find out the precise nature of the problems arising from the use of alternatives to interrogation, and which nevertheless result in adequate evidence being available, since these must be weighed in the balance against any loss of individual rights experienced by suspects under interrogation.

In the New Haven Study the authors say: 'The amount of evidence to convince a jury is not entirely predictable. Several law enforcement officials have suggested to us that considerably less evidence is often needed to convict a suspect than an observer would think, especially if the defendant had a prior record.'[2] However, they note that others have expressed contrary opinions: 'there is always a seed of doubt that remains until the defendant . . . rises and admits his guilt'. Despite this uncertainty as to how much evidence is required, the authors claim that in a sample of 90 cases, interrogation was successful in producing a confession or incriminating statement in 49 cases, but only necessary to the solution of 4 of the 49. 'In all other cases where information was obtained there was enough evidence prior to the questioning to convict the suspect' (p.1589).

As mentioned above, discussions with police officers in this country suggest that apart from the uncertainty relating to evidential material (and the belief in the personal advantage to be gained by high clearance rates), the primary reason for 'needing' a confession is to save time; as one officer put it: 'two hours spent getting a confession can save you five in court'.[3] If more effective investigative techniques were to be developed and used, it seems likely that considerable additional resources would be required, in particular budgetary increases to provide more and better trained police officers, improved

---

[1] See, for example, Sobel's (1966) study; he reported that interrogation and confession were vital in only about 10 per cent of serious felony indictments. Wald *et al* (1967) report on a number of studies which imply that investigative alternatives to interrogation are successfully used by law enforcement agencies. See note 161, p.1580.

[2] Under English law the prior record of the defendant would not normally be known by the jury until after the trial.

[3] It should be noted that many commentators have referred to the fact that even a small increase in the proportion of contested trials can present enormous difficulties for the administration of the court system. See, for example, Bottoms and McClean (1976), especially Chapter 1.

scientific equipment and additional back-up services for recording and processing data, not to mention an expanded court system.[1] In other words, if improved law enforcement is to be the primary aim of the police, i.e. catching and convicting more criminals, then they are correct in saying they need more resources.[2]

Finally, as Laurie (1970) points out, there are good sociological and psychological reasons for the police wanting confessions. 'The detective's *amour-propre* is involved. A guilty plea recognises the rightness of his case and the soundness of his judgment . . . The detective is as much a prisoner of the judicial system as the man he arrests. A guilty plea unties his hands and helps create a good relationship between them. As well as saving him a great deal of physical work, the guilty plea relieves him of a lot of worry and thought' (p.192). It also plays an important part in reinforcing perceptions of the detective's skill and credibility amongst his colleagues.

---

[1] The North American literature indicates that wide use can be made of computer technology which appears to be a highly successful means of achieving savings in personnel and time. See, for example, Cronkhite (1974).

[2] This is to ignore such other functions of policing as referral, prevention, and public education, all of which may be more effective means of crime control than is law enforcement through criminal investigation.

CHAPTER 3

The process of interrogation: theory and practice

'The tension between law and reality in present police practice is nowhere more apparent than in the area of custodial investigation', The Law Reform Commission of Australia, (1975, p.3).

Police powers: the unique position of the police

In the United States, Wilson (1968) argues that 'the law is one resource among many that he [the policeman] may use to deal with disorder', and he goes on to point out that the law does not provide positive instruction as to what an officer should do in any particular situation. In this country too, the laws and rules governing police questioning are thought to be a compromise between facilitating the conviction of criminals and ensuring fair treatment for suspects, so that the innocent are not convicted.

As was pointed out earlier, the police exercise a high degree of discretion with regard to crimes they will or will not investigate and which persons they will or will not question; but once the decision to investigate has been made, the law provides the police with a great deal of power, notwithstanding the fact that the rules governing their actions are often ambiguous.[1]

Two Canadians, Shearing and Leon (1977), refer to the fact that the law provides the police with *special* (their italics) access to law enforcement powers, and that these powers are unique to them. They further argue that the police have special access to a second resource which is not legitimately available to others, namely physical force. As Bittner (1975) points out '. . . what matters is that police procedure is defined by the feature that it may not be opposed in its course, and that force can be used if it is opposed'.[2]

Shearing and Leon go on to point out that *everything* (their italics) that a policeman does takes place within the context of the police licence and capability derived from the legitimacy of law enforcement *and* physical force.

---

[1] A *Times* leading article (9 September 1968) comments: 'The police are more than an instrument for enforcing law and order. They are a symbol of the authority that upholds law and order and for the majority they are the most conspicuous and ubiquitous symbol of that authority.'

[2] Bittner does not intend to imply that policemen make undue use of this resource, simply that its availability is central to the police role and differentiates it from the role of others.

This licence acts as a backdrop to all his activities and must be taken into account by any participants involved with the police – in the present context, questioning. If Shearing and Leon are correct, then although it is true that citizens are not legally obliged to answer the questions of police officers, nor are they obliged to go, or to remain in a police station unless they have been arrested, even if the policeman exerts no overt pressure and no reference is made to law enforcement or to the use of force, there is little doubt in either party's mind that there is always a possibility that resort will be made to one or other (or both) of these measures.

Whilst recognising the legitimacy of the primacy of the law enforcement role, The National Advisory Commission on Criminal Justice Standards and Goals (1973) appears less convinced that all participants are aware of this power differential, and it suggests that the effectiveness of the police is often dependent upon 'the participant's belief that the police have more authority than they actually have' (p.14).

A further point that needs to be borne in mind when considering the authority of the police (in terms of their capability to use the resources referred to by Shearing and Leon) lies in the likelihood of this authority being supported by other powerful groups, for example the judiciary. 'The "authority" of the policeman consists of the probability that his action will be backed up by other concentrations of power and it is limited because the conditions under which others will back him up are limited' (Stinchcombe, 1968).

Police-citizen encounters

The point at which 'questioning' or 'interviewing' becomes 'interrogation' is difficult, if not impossible, to determine. It therefore seems useful to refer to two sociological theories which help to explain police-citizen encounters, since whatever the outcome of this initial encounter – whether it leads to custody, arrest and interrogation, or whether it results in the citizen being allowed to resume his normal life – the first stages of the interaction will be crucial in terms of cooperation or conflict.[1]

The first study, by Wiley and Hudik (1974) views the interrogation as a two-way exchange between a police officer and a citizen, and argues that two factors are crucial in influencing the amount of cooperation given by the citizen. His cooperation is seen as being a 'reward' to the police officer, and is therefore dependent upon the value placed by him on the actions of the police; thus citizens are more cooperative when a reason is given for the interrogation, this being regarded as reducing the disutility (cost) and raising the utility (reward) of the exchange for them.[2] Cooperation further increases when the reason given reflects a police activity that is viewed as appropriate and

---

[1] Limitations of time prevented a fuller survey of the sociological literature on police-citizen encounters. See also Hartjen (1972) and Niederhoffer (1967).
[2] For a review of the literature on social exchange theory see Bredemeir (1977).

valuable by members of the community – for example citizens are more cooperative in investigations of crime against persons than victimless crimes.

The empirical research undertaken to test these hypotheses was carried out in a predominantly black poverty area in Chicago. Two hundred interviews were held with persons having the same characteristics as those most commonly stopped for interrogation in that area, and data were obtained on a further 200 interrogations carried out in the normal way by one of the authors (a police officer). The fieldwork clearly supported the hypotheses. 'If the citizen acts in a negative or abusive manner, policemen are likely to respond in kind. However, the officer often sets the tone for the interaction. A positive relationship can be established by such simple and low cost behaviour as providing explanations.'

Sheley and Harris (1976) question the interpretation given to the findings and suggest instead that 'it is not the reward value of cooperation, but rather the cost value of non-cooperation that is increased for the citizen'. Which of these interpretations is correct is an empirical matter which requires further research; however as Sheley and Harris point out, the question is not simply an academic one because if Wiley and Hudik are correct, the apparent civility and good faith shown by the policeman who gives reasons for his actions may be an important factor in law enforcement.

A second sociological theory which may help to explain police-citizen encounters is that of Sykes and Clark (1975) who examine the *mutual* (their italics) relations between both parties. Although they do not reject essentially psychological explanations of police behaviour (i.e. those based on working personality or prejudice), they suggest that a sociological explanation which stresses the importance of the rules which order police relations with civilians, and which are usually mutually acknowledged by both parties, is more fundamental. They refer specifically to the importance of the unequal status evident in many relationships between police and citizen. Police are of higher status than many with whom they interact by virtue of their occupational role and their socio-economic position. The authors hypothesize that many writers have failed fully to appreciate the extent to which this difference in status influences the flow of deference.

Sykes' and Clark's fieldwork was based on observation of 1466 encounters between police officers and citizens, in which some 9000 citizens were involved.[1] The research indicated that (a) as citizen status declined, so did the level of deference; (b) the amount of deference displayed by police officers was less than that displayed by citizens; and (c) exchanges between the police and non-white civilians were characterized by more mutual misunderstanding and disrespect and less mutual deference than encounters between the police and white civilians. Both these findings and those of Wiley and Hudick have as much relevance to the understanding of police encounters with non-whites in this country as in the United States.

Miller (1977) suggests that structural differences between the New York police and the London police have an important effect on their roles. The

---

[1] For details of methodology and a fuller discussion of their findings, see Sykes and Clark (1975).

London police are said to carry the weight of impersonal and institutional authority; for the New York police however, authority is said to be far more personal and political, and as a result, civilians are more willing to challenge police authority.[1] It is however, crucial to bear in mind that structural differences between the police in the two countries should not be allowed to obscure the importance of American research findings for this country, especially where they concern the interaction between police and citizens, as distinct from purely organisational factors.

Techniques of interrogation

There seems little doubt that police officers in England and Wales receive little training in interrogative techniques. Only a small part of the time at detective training school is devoted to such skills; instead there is said to be a heavy concentration of instruction on the law relating to specific (and often obscure) offences.

Most of the manuals and texts on the subject are American, but there is no evidence that they are actually read by detectives in this country. In England and Wales, the interrogation of suspects is dealt with by the *Judges' Rules* and the *Administrative Directions on Interrogation and the Taking of Statements,* both issued in 1964.[2]

All of the American manuals cover much the same ground. The investigator is urged to acquaint himself thoroughly with all the background information to the case prior to interrogation. He should have absolute control over the interrogation process both psychologically and physically. Privacy is said to be the best means of dominance over a suspect. The room in which interrogation takes place should be sparsely furnished, and in some cases soft lighting, two-way mirrors and recording apparatus are recommended. Deprivation of family, friends, and counsel is considered very important as a means of ensuring both that the atmosphere is authoritarian and that the interrogator becomes the nearest thing to a 'friend' (the implication being that we all need friends, and in the absence of any alternative, even the police interrogator becomes a friend). It is perhaps best summed up by O'Hara (1973): 'The atmosphere suggests the invincibility of the forces of law'.[3]

---

[1] Monkkonen (1977) draws attention to some methodological weaknesses in Miller's work, in particular the fact that whilst written sources were available for the London police, he was forced to rely upon non-comparable published reports and newspaper accounts for the New York police. Monkkonen comments: 'Miller's analysis rings true, but must remain speculative'.

[2] *Editorial note:* the Rules and Directions were reissued in 1978 to take account of relevant Home Office circulars issued since 1964. See *Judges' Rules and Administrative Directions to the Police.* Home Office Circular No 89/1978, London, HMSO.

[3] A very detailed survey of both the police science and the social science suggestions covering the tactics of interrogation is to be found in Driver (1968). For other texts see, for example, Mettler (1977); Wicks (1974); Reiser (1973); Royal and Schutt (1976); Inbau and Reid (1967). Similar views are expressed in the Australian and New Zealand Literature; see for example, Crowley (1973) and Gordon (1964).

One other feature of many texts and manuals is their stress on the fact that interrogation is an art, although as Gordon (1964) adds, it is regarded as 'an art well within the ability of every police officer and can be achieved by diligent application and study of a particularly interesting subject'.

Deeley (1971), one of the few British writers to discuss in considerable detail the techniques used in interrogation in England and Wales, suggests that English and American detectives approach interrogation from opposite ends of the job. 'For an English policeman there is little tuition, apart from lectures during his initial training, and a refresher talk on promotion . . . he learns his skills on the job, at the elbow of a senior man. The British attitude, in a phrase, is that a good interrogator is born in heaven, not taught' (p.140).

The police journals in this country add little in the way of further advice. Goodsall (1974), writing in the *Police Review* advises that keeping the initiative, displaying tact and patience and being fully conversant with the law and with the facts of the case will bring results from an interrogation. Firth (1975), writing in the same journal reiterates this advice and stresses the need for patience, persistence and 'the gift of the gab'. Firth's article is particularly interesting because there are so few references in the literature to the interrogation of children. He comments: 'Children are far better at perfecting the lie than adults. They are more convincing and the danger is that they will convince an inexperienced officer . . . The interrogator is at a disadvantage when he is required [by the Judges' Rules] to have a parent or guardian present.' He adds that children will usually offer part of a story and hope the interrogator will accept it, but the interrogator should press on, even though some of the guilt has been admitted. Finally, Firth notes 'that as drops of water dripping on a stone will gradually wear it away so interrogation will achieve results.'

The legal position in England and Wales and proposals for change

As the law stands at present it is unlawful to detain a person for the sole purpose of questioning, and citizens are not legally obliged to answer the questions of police officers, nor to go, or remain, in a police station unless they have been arrested. As has been pointed out by Ashworth (1976), in practice very few people refused to accompany the police to the station when 'invited' to do so;[1] if more people effectively insisted on their liberties in this regard, Ashworth argues that 'the police would be greatly handicapped in their crime detecting function' (p.495), though he adds that there might possibly be some gain to the cause of 'justice'.

Insofar as the person concerned agrees voluntarily to be questioned, the police may do so until such time as they either release him, or there is sufficient evidence to warrant his being charged. These procedures are set out in the Judges' Rules, originally issued in 1912 and revised in 1918 and 1964, and the Administrative Directions which supplement the Rules.[2]

---

[1] Some of the possible explanations for this are discussed earlier in this chapter, under 'Police powers' and 'Police-citizen encounters'.

[2] See above, p.18 fn.

Very briefly, the 1964 Rules can be summed up as follows:[1]

a. The police may question any person about the commission of an offence whether or not the person has been taken into custody, and may do so long as he has not been charged with the offence or informed that he may be prosecuted for it.

b. As soon as the police have evidence which affords reasonable grounds for suspecting that a person has committed an offence he must be cautioned before further questioning.

c. When a person is charged with, or informed that he may be prosecuted for an offence, he must be cautioned.

d. If a person chooses to make a written statement he must be allowed to do so without prompting. If he chooses to dictate a statement, it must be taken down verbatim and without prompting.

e. When more than one offender has been charged, a statement made by one may be put before the other(s), but with no suggestion that any reply or comment be made. Before any such comment is made, the person must again be cautioned.

f. Persons other than police officers charged with investigating offences or charging offenders must comply with the Rules.

The Rules are prefaced by a number of general principles which include two important additional points:

a. 'That every person at any stage of an investigation shall be able to communicate and to consult privately with a solicitor . . . provided . . . no unreasonable delay or hindrance is caused to the process of investigation or the administration of justice by his doing so.

b. 'That it is a fundamental condition of the admissibility in evidence against any person, equally of any oral answer given by that person . . . and of any statement made by that person, that it shall have been voluntary, in the sense that it has not been obtained from him by fear of prejudice or hope of advantage, exercised or held out by a person in authority, or by oppression.'

The last mentioned principle is regarded as overriding and applicable in all cases. 'Non-conformity with the Rules may render answers and statements liable to be excluded from evidence in subsequent criminal procedings.'

Since the 1964 revision of the Rules, they have come under increasing criticism, and are the subject of considerable legal argument.[2] However, it is perhaps worth noting that even at the time of their issue many lawyers were unhappy. Thomas (1964), for example, comments: 'apart from the ambiguous legal status of the Judges' Rules themselves, the decision of the Court of Criminal Appeal in *Waterfield*[3] reveals how defective the law is in *general*

---

[1] Only the barest outline is given here; more details will emerge as the report goes on to discuss the various comments and criticisms that have been levelled at the Rules in recent years. For a full account of the historical background, the Rules themselves, and subsequent controversies see Wegg-Prosser (1973), especially Chapter 5.

[2] The following account of the criticisms of the Rules draws heavily on the account given by Wegg-Prosser, *op cit.*

[3] [1963] 3 All E.R. 659.

principle (emphasis added) and the law of arrest remains as chaotic as ever. The revision of the Judges' Rules should be regarded as the first step in the process of rationalising the law of criminal investigation on the basis of modern police methods' (p.386).

Twelve years later, Ashworth (1976) makes a similar point. 'Criminal investigation is an area of paramount constitutional significance and yet, in England as elsewhere, the actual conduct of investigation by police and other agencies is known to bear little relation to the written Rules. The law becomes of little relevance to real events, the course of which may come to be dictated by the strengths of the parties' (p.594).

In 1967, a Committee of Justice, the British section of the International Commission of Jurists, produced a written report on the interrogation of suspects. The Committee recommended some fundamental changes in the Rules. It referred to police complaints that the Rules seriously hampered their investigations and it therefore advised that the right of the accused to remain silent should be abolished. However, in order to safeguard the accused, the Committee also proposed that any confession of guilt should not be admissible in evidence unless it was made, and recorded, in front of a magistrate, or tape-recorded by the police. Furthermore, the Committee recommended that legal aid and advice should be available to suspects before questioning.

Other critics of the Rules included Lord Parker, then the Lord Chief Justice, who, in 1970, proposed the abolition of the caution. Both this recommendation, and those of Justice were criticized by Mr Justice McKenna. He strongly defended the retention of the accused's right to silence, but supported interrogation before a magistrate.

In 1971, Lord Parker's successor as Lord Chief Justice, Lord Widgery, suggested that remaining silent should no longer be regarded as something respectable, but should require explanation and be a matter from which the jury might draw adverse inferences. That same year, Professor Rupert Cross put forward a view similar to that of Lord Widgery; he described the right to silence as a 'sacred cow'. Commenting on these views in its issue of September 1971, the editor of the *Criminal Law Review* thought that they overstated the case and doubted whether the right to silence impeded police investigation to any great extent.

In 1972, Sir Robert Mark, at that time Commissioner of Police of the Metropolis, expressed concern about the increase in serious crime and the high rate of acquittals. He quoted with approval Glanville Williams' (1963) comment that 'a rule giving excessive protection to an accused person becomes even less defensible as the criminal law turns to remedial treatment instead of punishment'. Sir Robert thought changes in the Rules should include the abandonment of the right to silence.

The Criminal Law Revision Committee's Eleventh Report on Evidence was published in 1972. The Committee had been asked to review the law of evidence in criminal cases and to consider whether changes were desirable in the interests of the fair and efficient administration of justice. Its Report, like the original Rules, has since aroused tremendous controversy.

The Committee assumed that the present adversarial system would continue, as would trial by jury. But it felt that the Judges' Rules were not necessary in the 1970s and the idea that the accused had 'a sacred right to the benefit of anything in the law which gives a chance of acquittal, however strong the case against him' was not an acceptable one. As a consequence, the Committee proposed to restrict the suspect's right to silence when questioned by the police. He would retain the right only insofar as it would be no offence to refuse to answer questions, but would run the risk that, at trial, as adverse inference might be drawn from his silence.

It follows from this that the caution would be abolished. The Committee recommended that it should be replaced by a written warning informing the accused of the charge, and pointing out that if, during questioning, he failed to mention a fact upon which he afterwards relied for his defence, the court or jury might draw whatever inferences it thought proper.

The Committee rejected as impractical suggestions of interrogation before a magistrate. It viewed the idea of tape-recording interrogations in a much more favourable light, although only a minority (three members) favoured the compulsory use of such equipment. It recommended that confessions obtained by oppressive treatment should continue to be inadmissible unless it could be proved that the threat or inducement did not make the confession unreliable.[1]

The relevance of the Criminal Law Revision Committee's recommendations for the Judges' Rules

The fact that since its publication (and even before) there have been endless legal debates over the issues raised by the Criminal Law Revision Committee's Report, is probably far less important than the fact that its recommendations were posited upon the assumption that the Judges' Rules were, or even could be, adhered to in practice. It is well recognised that the Rules are notoriously imprecise and ambiguous (see, for example, Glasbeek and Prentice, 1968). Furthermore, they were intended for the *guidance* of police officers, and have never had the force of law. A barrister, writing in the *Criminal Law Review* in 1967 comments that the Rules might be useful if they are complied with, but he claims they are not, and their very existence gives rise to allegations that police officers commit perjury. The police are said to disobey the Rules when they feel that it is in the interests of obtaining a conviction, and the author ends by quoting a police officer who said: 'Any police officer who doesn't know the Judges' Rules is a fool, but he would be even more of a fool if he adhered to them' (p.94).

The legal journals are full of articles making this same point or similar ones; criticisms of the way the Rules are by-passed in practice are legion. The authors of these articles, usually end by either demanding that the Rules be abolished, (some authors would like them replaced by new ones), or drastically revised.

Very little empirical work has been done to determine what goes on in practice. However, those who *have* had an opportunity to observe

---

[1] The Committee also dealt with other matters, but these fall outside the scope of this report.

interrogations in practice seem to agree that there has been a change over the past 10 or 15 years in the way the Rules are applied. The reasons for this are not clear, but it has been suggested that it results from (a) police officers' greater awareness of the Rules; (b) greater professionalism of the service; and (c) the growing importance of the complaints procedure in police work. A fourth, rather more subjective or impressionistic reason that has been advanced concerns the youth and inexperience of a great many police officers today; they do not have the years of experience and confidence which are needed before they can know just how far they can go before getting into serious trouble. If these comments are valid, it is somewhat paradoxical that the public have become more aware of the problems in the CID at a time when the pressures on the police to conform to the Rules have become so much greater.

Discussions with researchers who have been able to observe interrogations as part of wider research projects have raised some very interesting issues which seem crucial to any consideration of change, or abandonment of, the Judges' Rules. Furthermore, they confirm many of the more theoretical writings of lawyers. In the first place, it has been suggested that the Rules were formulated largely in a vacuum and that for all practical purposes they are unrealistic. Both the pre-trial procedure and what goes on in court represent a kind of dishonest game – everyone knows that the situation being described is not *quite* what happened, but because the game is played within certain rules, it is accepted. The Rules are a statement of what people *ought* to be doing at a particular stage of the investigation; whether it is possible for the investigating officer to comply with them is not really considered. For example, during the course of questioning, a witness may become a suspect and his status *vis-à-vis* the police may change. The officer's thoughts must necessarily be on what questions he is going to ask (or refrain from asking), without revealing that he knows less than he implies; his concern is to obtain information that will be of evidential value in court.[1] At the same time, under the Judges' Rules, he must consider at what stage he ought to be cautioning the suspect – a situation which he must see as almost extraneous to the real object of interrogation. Identifying this point in time demands a lot of an officer. As Thompson (1967) points out: 'It seems absurd to ask a police officer to charge a suspect as soon as he has enough evidence to do so, bringing to an end his freedom to interrogate and having to warn the suspect that he need volunteer no further information' (p.100).

A further problem arises in respect of the concepts underlying the Rules and the language in which they are couched. For example, the word 'caution' in the sense that it is used in the Rules dropped out of usage in the 19th century–the word 'warn' is now common parlance. One result of this situation is that the Rules are in fact 'translated', and a great deal is left to the discretion of the individual officer as to how this is done. Despite this, and because of the authority of the police officer, the defendant inevitably tends to see

---

[1] Note the discrepancy here between the 'ideal' and the 'real'. All text books stress that the interrogator must know *in advance* how he will conduct the questioning.

the caution as a meaningless ritual, and his compliance is most likely to be the result of the perceived advantage of cooperation.

Finally, the Rules may be unrealistic because they do not differentiate between serious offences and petty offences. Whilst it is true that the police themselves deal with 'crime' and 'criminals' in a generalised sense, to expect them to process the shoplifter or the pickpocket in the same way as the murder suspect is undoubtedly flying in the face of reality.[1]

Three particular aspects of the Judges' Rules continue to be a cause of major concern: 'voluntary' confessions; access to a solicitor and legal advice; and the right to silence. These are discussed in turn below.

'Voluntary' statements and confessions

In the United States a good deal has been written about the compulsion to confess. Driver (1968) points out that even before interrogation, men tend to talk even when to do so is to their detriment, for the imbalance between the state and the accused begins with arrest and detention.[2] In the New Haven Study referred to earlier, it was reported that some uncoerced confessions were virtually spontaneous. Theodor Reik (1959) argues that men have a 'compulsive, unconscious tendency to confess' (p.180), but whatever the roots of such a compulsion, it is, as Driver points out 'almost certainly intensified by the host of fears generated by the situations and procedures of arrest and detention' (p.57).

Zimbardo (1967) examines the psychological tactics and techniques of interrogation as set out in manuals used to train detectives and he comments, 'I am convinced that these methods are psychologically coercive; that they deprive the individual if his human dignity and fundamental rights; and that they debase the police who use them . . . ' (p.19).

Arens and Meadow (1956) also discuss in some detail what they describe as third degree practices in the process of obtaining confessions in the United States. 'Acceptance of some of these pressures as "respectable" confession-getting devices under contemporary urban mores was strikingly displayed . . . when the prosecutor, in defending a confession as "voluntary" explained that it was readily obtained from a man who was "not hard to break".' The authors add that 'occasional judicial discovery of such travesties has not been effective in suppressing illegal police practices, but has succeeded only in driving them underground' (p.21). One writer, however, suggests that the psychological aspects of secret interrogation are less damaging to a person's mental health than are the stresses of everyday life (Marx, 1952).

In this country, Glanville Williams (1960) quotes Wigmore: 'The nervous pressure of guilt is enormous; the load of the deed done is heavy; the fear of

---

[1] In France, for example, a distinction is made between crimes and less serious infractions so far as arrest and detention are concerned (see James, 1977 p.308).

[2] In England and Wales it could be said to start even earlier, namely at the stage where a person is 'invited' to 'help the police with their enquiries'.

detection fills the consciousness; when detection comes the pressure is relieved; and the deep sense of relief makes confession a satisfaction' (p.334 – 5).

It might be helpful if more were known about the type of person who does and who does not confess, but no research of this nature appears to have been undertaken in this country. In the United States, Neubauer (1974) found that defendants accused of property crimes were much more likely to confess than those accused of crimes against the person. He explains these different confession rates in terms of the persuasiveness of the evidence that can be used to convince the suspect that a denial is hopeless. Neubauer also concludes from an examination of defendants' age, bail status and type of attorney, that 'there is no evidence to prove the proposition that disadvantaged groups are more likely to confess' (p.111). He argues that this result is consistent with the findings of two other studies (Leiken, 1970; Griffiths and Ayres, 1967) which found that the propensity to confess was unrelated to the educational level of suspects.

'Voluntary' incriminating statements may be made because the police officer and the suspect both want something out of the situation; as a result, the suspect may talk in order to strike what he perceives as the best bargain. If this is indeed the case, it is probable that police officers will, within a very short space of time, run the risk of breaking the Rules. Without detailed observational studies, the extent to which this happens is impossible to estimate, but bargaining theory, when combined with the power differential between the two persons involved would certainly help to explain the fact that only exceptionally are 'third degree' tactics resorted to by the police. For the most part, the give and take implicit in an encounter is sufficient to ensure that each of the parties believes they are gaining something from it; no promises need to be made, no favours given, there is simply a built-in assumption which is understood by both parties that certain decisions remain flexible and may be influenced by the outcome of the interrogation.[1] The points are important since, if the Rules are indeed 'bent' in these or in other ways, the courts may view the resulting evidence as inadmissible.[2, 3]

The nub of the problem lies in the police officer's need for a confession in order to provide evidence of guilt. The Law Reform Commission of Australia (1975) draws attention to the fact that 'the outcome of the criminal trial will often turn upon the facts relating to the obtaining of the alleged confession and the terms in which the confession is allegedly made' (para. 154). The

---

[1] For a discussion of police discretion and the potential for negotiation see Bottoms and McClean (1976), especially Chapters 5 and 8.

[2] It has been suggested that real tension exists during interrogations in serious cases. On the one hand the officer is anxious that his evidence should not be challenged in court since he regards it as important to secure a conviction, both for the sake of public protection and in order to avoid any criticism of his own behaviour. In order to ensure this, officers claim to be scrupulous in their methods of interrogation. On the other hand, the interrogation may not proceed in a manner that satisfies the officer's need for evidence and so he is tempted to bend the Rules. The dilemma creates a tightrope for the officer who needs strong evidence, or better still a confession, in order to avoid a trial at court.

[3] In conversation with police officers I was told that the police do not consider that they 'bend' even the intent of the law; the Rules are so vague and imprecise that they have no need to.

Commission also points out that where there is no confession, police reliance on 'verballing' is 'so widespread as to warrant . . . a limitation on the admissibility of alleged confessions' (para 155). Without adequate research, it is impossible to say to what extent such comments are applicable to this country.

Unfortunately, there is little empirical information regarding the frequency with which disputes arise in relation to 'verbals' or confessions, nor about the particular aspects of the interrogation process over which they occur.[1] A Home Office Report, *The Feasibility of an Experiment in the Tape Recording of Police Interrogations* includes some data about challenges to oral and written statements derived from studies carried out by the Metropolitan Police and by the Kent and South Wales police forces in 1973 and 1975. The studies indicate that challenges were rare in cases tried at magistrates' courts and not common, although they occurred proportionately more frequently, in cases tried in the Crown Court. This is not a surprising finding in view of the more serious nature of the offences in the higher courts.

If the theories advanced by Driver (1968), Reik (1959), Zimbardo (1967) and others are accepted, then there is little justification for regarding any statement or confession as entirely 'voluntary. The nature and atmosphere of the interrogation process would seem to obviate such a possibility, and coercion, if not duress, is implicit in the situation. This suggests that far-reaching changes would be necessary if self-incrimination is to be avoided. The three which have received most attention in recent years are the use of tape recordings; the exclusionary rule; and interrogation before a magistrate. These proposals are discussed later in this chapter; mention of them here is not intended to imply that any of them would resolve the problem satisfactorily.

Access to a solicitor and legal advice

It is surely significant that the Eleventh Report of the Criminal Law Revision Committee makes no reference to the suspect's right of access to a solicitor (see Morton, 1972). The word 'significant' is used deliberately because the issue is one of the most substantive ones surrounding the interrogation process, insofar as it underlies the problem of the right to silence which has, by contrast, received widespread attention.[2] The Judges' Rules state that 'every person at any stage of an investigation, should be able to communicate and to consult privately with a solicitor . . . provided . . . no unreasonable delay or hindrance is caused to the process of investigation or the administration of justice by his doing so'. It is, of course, the latter part of this direction that highlights the controversy which surrounds the question of access. Leigh

---

[1] On the issue of 'verbals' see Morton (1975).
[2] One reason for this is that the argument about the right to silence is largely theoretical. The right of access to a solicitor (and the associated question of legal aid) is very much more a *practical* concern and one which could, without too much difficulty, be put into effect were it not for the unresolved philosophical arguments which surround the question of the right to silence.

(1975) notes that the direction imposes no obligation on the police to allow a solicitor to be present either before or during interrogation, a situation which differs in an important way from many other jurisdictions where access is found at common law or under statute. Zander (1972a) adds to this comment by drawing attention to the fact that 'the courts never seem to have given authoritative guidance as to what constitutes circumstances that justify the police in refusing a suspect his "right" to speak to his lawyers. In the absence of any ruling by the courts it would not be surprising to find that it was being given a broad interpretation by the police in their own favour' (p.342 – 3).

In 1972, Zander carried out two studies to discover the extent to which suspects were allowed to consult a solicitor in police stations (Zander 1972a, 1972b). In the first, he interviewed 132 prisoners who had appealed to the Court of Appeal. Fifty seven of them said they had asked to see a solicitor and 42 (74 per cent) of these said permission had been refused. Zander reports that many of those who had not asked to see a solicitor subsequently regretted their decision and put it down to ignorance of their rights, 'nerves' etc.

In a second study, carried out the same year, Zander sent questionnaires to 54 police stations in the Metropolitan Police District in order to discover the extent to which they provided facilities which might assist suspects to know, and use their legal rights. In roughly 9 out of 10 replies the police said that they would help a suspect to find a solicitor, but in view of the findings reported above, Zander concludes that 'it seems probable that those who answered in the affirmative meant, by their response that, *if* (emphasis added) they allowed the suspect to consult a solicitor, they would give him assistance in getting to one'. Zander continues, 'I do not interpret this response to mean that they would necessarily permit such access'.

The observations in the *Report of an Inquiry by the Hon Sir Henry Fisher into the circumstances leading to the trial of three persons on charges arising out of the death of Maxwell Confait and the fire at 27 Doggett Road, London SE6* (henceforth referred to as the *Confait* Report) lend support to Zander's conjectures about the absence of facilities for advising suspects of their rights. Fisher writes, 'the evidence . . . was that notices are displayed in police stations in the Metropolitan Police District, but in practice persons in custody are *not* informed orally of the rights and facilities available to them, nor is their attention drawn to the notices'. Fisher obtained his information from the Deputy Assistant Commissioner (Crime), Metropolitan Police, who stated, 'all I can say in all honesty is that if there is a duty to inform every person in custody orally that he has a right to consult a solicitor before we commence the interview, then in practice we do not do it . . . It has never been regarded by the police . . . as a duty to tell a prisoner . . . that he has a right to consult a solicitor.'

The most controversial context in which the question of access to counsel has been argued relates to the question of the suspect's right to silence. It is postulated (not only by the police themselves) that if a lawyer were to be present during questioning, the police would be unable to perform their law enforcement task since any sensible lawyer would, from the outset, advise his client to say nothing. Against this it has been argued that the presence of a lawyer would have no greater effect than to put the recipients of his advice in

27

the same position as better informed and more sophisticated suspects; it is the ignorant and weaker members of society who are placed at greatest disadvantage by the present procedure.

Apart from the question of avoiding self-incrimination, a number of other reasons for the presence of a lawyer have been put forward; he may, for example, advise suspects of their options in relation to identification parades, finger-printing, medical tests and photographs. A lawyer can also advise on applications for bail, and on detainees' rights in respect of the length of time they can be held without being charged. Finally, his presence may ensure generally fair treatment by the police and, no less important, act as a psychological support for the citizen whether he be a witness or a suspect.

It is, of course, important to recognise that any changes in the Judges' Rules which would permit a wider use of legal advice must necessarily involve serious attention to the availability of solicitors. Whilst it is widely held that in some cases the police do not exert much effort to find a lawyer, it must also be pointed out that despite the extension of Duty Solicitor schemes and the expansion of Law Centres, it is often difficult to obtain the services of a lawyer at odd hours of the night or at weekends.[1] There is usually no problem when the solicitor is being paid out of private funds, but those paid under the Legal Aid and Assistance Scheme seem to be less readily available.

Fisher deals with this question in general in the *Confait* Report (pp.184 – 186). He examined particulars of Duty Solicitor schemes, the arrangements made by Law Centres, by Release, and by the Citizens' Advice Bureaux and he concludes that 'it would in general be difficult to get a solicitor after 6 pm'. He also draws attention to *R v Tullett*[2] from which it appears that costs incurred prior to the grant of a legal aid order can be taxed and paid. On this ruling, a solicitor who attends a police station at the request of an indigent accused can obtain payment for these services provided that a legal aid order is subsequently made. But he is not able to do so if the police decide to make no charge.

The right to silence

The right to silence exists in two quite distinct situational contexts, and it is important to distinguish between them, for although the right against *self-incrimination* is a matter of general principle, detailed arguments for and against the right to silence necessarily differ depending upon whether the right is exercised in the police station by a *suspect,* or in court by an *accused.* This is because the silence of a suspect may have a very different meaning from the silence of an accused, and because the relationship between a policeman and a suspect will be very different from that existing between the court and an accused. In this report, consideration is given only to the exercise of the right to silence in the police station, but it should be noted that in much of the

---

[1] This is also the case with local authority social workers, a situation that often affects the interrogation of juveniles in the care of such authorities.
[2] [1976] 1 WLR 241.

literature the arguments advanced are, implicitly if not explicitly, assumed to apply to both contexts, as is the empirical evidence, where this is available.

Earlier discussion of the 'compulsion' to confess, and of the need that both interrogator and suspect have to bargain with each other, as well as the inadequacy of access to legal counsel, must lead to the conclusion that in practice the right to silence is more myth than reality. It is, however, an issue which has been extremely controversial for many years. Briefly, those who wish to abolish the right claim that it does no more than help the guilty. It is said that abolition of the right would rationalise the law and excuse the courts from drawing absurdly fine distinctions for juries; and it is suggested that abolition would not be oppressive in practice in that the inference of guilt would not be automatic, but would have to be reasonable in the circumstances and determined by a jury in the light of all the evidence. Finally, and perhaps most stridently, it has been argued that the right of silence has resulted in high acquittal rates for serious crimes, and lower prosecution and conviction rates.[1] The main arguments advanced by those in favour of retaining the right are that there are social reasons for silence which are perfectly consistent with innocence and that if inferences can be drawn from silence, suspects will be forced to speak.[2]

In this country, empirical work on the subject is thin on the ground. Bottoms and McClean (1976) who interviewed nearly 300 defendants who appeared before Sheffield magistrates' court note that 70 per cent of them claimed that they told the police right from the start that they had committed the offence. Perhaps more important for the present discussion is the fact that a further 24 per cent admitted their guilt to the police at a later stage, and as the authors point out '. . . it is in this area that police interrogation practice is relevant'. There is no information about whether these suspects were told of their right to silence; Bottoms and McClean say only that 'the absence of legal representatives at the time of police interrogation leaves the suspect with the somewhat thin protection of the Judges' Rules . . .'

Greenawalt (1974) draws attention to the fact that most observers believe that in both England and Wales and in the United States there are substantial failures by the police to comply with the rules protecting silence. Referring specifically to England, he adds, 'since the police may wish to conceal violations, researchers cannot establish the precise degree of non-compliance, but close study of interactions between the police and suspects can certainly contribute to a more accurate picture of what takes place' (p.247). As has been apparent throughout this report, most of the published work on this subject comes from America. Zander's (1972a) research on the lack of access to solicitors at police stations is relevant, since if suspects are denied access they are more likely not to assert their right of silence, even assuming that they

---

[1] An excellent account of competing viewpoints is to be found in *The Right to Silence: Symposium.* Proceedings of the Institute of Criminology, University of Sydney. No. 17, 1973.

[2] This brief summary of the arguments illustrates how they fail to differentiate between the two contexts referred to above. For example, the argument that if the courts can draw inferences from silence, suspects will be forced to speak fails to distinguish between silence at the police station and silence at court.

know of it and understand the precise meaning of the caution. Such an assumption is questionable; Fisher, in the *Confait* Report draws attention to the ambiguity implicit in the wording of the caution. 'The second half of the caution (". . . but what you say may be put into writing and given in evidence") assumes that the person *does* talk and may well seem to a simple person to negate the first part, especially when followed by a question or an invitation to speak' (p.188). This latter point is also made by Glasbeek and Prentice (1968): '. . . a caution advising a suspect of his right to remain silent loses much of its authority when immediately followed by persistent questioning' (p.480). Nor does the caution mention that the suspect may, at his own request, terminate the interview, although this right is implicit in the right to silence.

Furthermore, even where warnings are given, American research suggests that this does not significantly inhibit the giving of 'voluntary' statements. Medalie, Zeitz and Alexander (1968) found that 40 per cent of a sample of defendants arrested after the Supreme Court's decision in *Miranda*[1] had voluntarily given statements to the police and they add: 'not only had some of the defendants misunderstood the warnings (regarding the right to remain silent and to have access to counsel), but even those who had a cognitive understanding of the warnings, nevertheless failed to appreciate the significance of the warnings and lacked the ability of applying them in the context of the specific arrest situation'.[2] Nonetheless, many commentators emphasise the fact that although the rights conferred by the *Miranda* rules do not significantly affect the number of suspects who talk 'voluntarily', the protection they afford the suspect is to be welcomed, since it makes for justice and fairness.

The right to silence is the concrete and visible assertion of the fundamental principle that the prosecution must prove their case and that no obligation lies on the accused to prove his or her innocence (see, for example, Miller, 1973). Few appear to have considered the rationale for protecting people from self-incrimination whilst at the same time operating with a judicial system which relies so heavily on admissions of guilt. So long as these remain conflicting demands within the system, it seems hardly surprising that ways are sought, and found, to circumvent the right to silence. Arguments for and against retaining it are couched in terms of individual rights versus the need to convict guilty people, but there is little discussion of alternative methods of obtaining the necessary evidence (for example, by improved policing skills) in order to reduce the importance of confessions.

On the issue of individual rights, the arguments for and against the right to silence are largely ethical and it seems that there is little likelihood of general agreement; value judgements are involved and the debate will doubtless reflect a wide spectrum of ideological perspectives and personal viewpoints. It may,

---

[1] See above p.4 fn.

[2] Others who refer to the ineffectiveness of the *Miranda* warnings include Seeburger and Wettick (1967) and Wald *et al* (1968). A particularly interesting account of how the police are able to subvert the *Miranda* warnings whilst technically complying with them is given by Lewis and Allen (1977). A good summary of American empirical work on *Miranda* is to be found in Pepinsky (1970).

therefore, be worth remembering the unequal nature of the power relationship in any encounter between policeman and suspect, as well as the 'normal' psychological pressure on the latter to talk and indeed to confess. Any limitation on the right to silence will almost certainly further increase this imbalance. There is little doubt that increased pressure to speak would result, by definition, in fewer instances of silence and more admissions and confessions; whether more innocent people would plead guilty to crimes they had not committed it is impossible to say.

The Judges' Rules. To enforce? To amend? To scrap?

Both academic and practising lawyers, as well as other informed and concerned persons remain highly critical of the Judges' Rules; most of the discussion has centred round the desirability or otherwise of retaining the Rules, and whether some or all of them should be modified. Many such arguments have been concerned with legal definitions − the difficulty of defining terms such as 'arrest' and 'custody'; others have been more philosophical in content, dealing with the conflict between the rights of suspects and the need for an 'orderly' society. Fisher, in the *Confait* Report argues that the Rules should be governed by law, on the grounds that 'the balance between the effectiveness of police investigations and the protection of the individual is important enough to be governed by law and that the consequences of a breach of the Rules should be clear and certain' (para 15.7).

All commentators seem generally agreed that the Rules are widely disregarded and it is this fact which appears to underlie the various proposals for change. However, neither those who would like to see them scrapped nor those who would like to see them given the force of law seem to think it necessary to question the *purpose* of the Rules. Their ambiguity is well recognised in relation to their operationalisation, but not in relation to what it is they are intended to achieve. Before making any rational decision as to either their effectiveness or their desirability, it would seem important to give consideration to these questions: do they exist for the protection of the suspect? or for the guidance of the police? or to assist the court in deciding what is or is not admissible? or a mixture of two or all of these?

There appears also to be some confusion in respect of people's views on the issue of legality; the fact that the Judges' Rules are not rules of law is well recognised, but in most discussions of them the implication seems to be that since the Rules exist, they *ought* to be enforced as though they were law, and breaches should be penalised by either the judiciary in court or by the police themselves through their discipline code. However, as Amsterdam (1974) points out, 'if there are no fairly clear rules telling the policeman what he may and may not do, courts are seldom going to say what he did was unreasonable' (p.394).

That it is widely expected that the Rules should be enforced is evidenced by by the way writers who have commented adversely on the fact that judges accept police evidence that is presented to them in court without enquiring how it was obtained, argue that since this is well known to the police, the latter are not too careful about their methods. Griffith (1977) points out that in respect of the enforcememt of the Judges' Rules the judiciary have 'a variable record' (p.85). A similar point is made by Keeton (1977) and by Williams (1961) who refers to the fact that the judges have given up enforcing their own rules 'for it is no longer the practice to exclude evidence illegally obtained by questioning in custody' (p.51). He adds: 'When judges both assert that the police should discipline themselves, and yet admit evidence that has been obtained by lack of the judicially imposed discipline, the stultification of our professions becomes patent.'

If, however, the Rules are recognised and acknowledged to be simply rules of practice rather than of law, then two important questions arise: on the one hand, to what extent is it legitimate to criticise the judiciary for not enforcing them as though they were law and on the other hand, by not ensuring their enforcement, is the judiciary, albeit tacitly, approving of improper behaviour?

If, indeed, the *intent* is that they should be rules of law, then it may be argued that appropriate action should be taken by Parliament, and there seems little point in proposing halfway measures which simply involve modifications by rewording the Rules, and changing their method of publication and dissemination. Given the present absence of any outside control over interrogation practices, it is difficult to see how even modified Rules are to be enforced 'voluntarily', i.e. without giving them the force of law. On the other hand, the question must arise as to whether giving the Rules the force of law is the most satisfactory means of controlling police activities. Driver (1968) argues that the 'subtle forces' which operate even in interrogations which are subject to proper legal controls are so great, and so much part of the situation of interrogation that 'ameliorating safeguards seem futile: effective measures to right the imbalance created by the "inherently coercive" atmosphere might be no less than tantamount to the abolition of the institution' (p.61).

The manuals available in the United States on techniques of interrogation lead one to suppose the procedures considered 'normal' in that country may be quite exceptional in England and Wales, and this may explain the milder tone adopted by Glanville Williams (1960): '. . . complete prohibition of the questioning of those who are strongly suspected is difficult to enforce . . . and if it were strictly enforced might breed cynicism. The police might well ask themselves whether society can be so interested in the conviction of offenders, if it withholds from the officers of the law one of the most potent means (and often the only means) of obtaining the evidence necessary for a conviction.'

Whether the Judges' Rules are abolished or modified, there remains the question of how the powers of the police are to be controlled. This is put succinctly by Amsterdam (1974). 'I can think of few issues more important to a society than the amount of power that it permits its police to use without effective control by law' (p.377). Later in the same paper, he asks, 'how are administrable rules to be fashioned that protect those who do not want to be hassled by the police from being hassled, while permitting the police sufficient leeway to make contact with citizens . . . for all the numerous purposes for which such contacts may be necessary?' One answer, he suggests is the introduction of new regulatory devices, principally police rulemaking, which can be effectively overseen by the courts.

Control of police activities

Three means of exercising control over police activities have been the subject of considerable debate: the use of recording machines; the exclusionary rule; and interrogation before a magistrate. Each of these issues is dealt with below.

The use of tape and video recordings

Although a majority of the Criminal Law Revision Committee favoured wider use of tape recorders during interrogation, it was reluctant to recommend their general use without experimental assessment of the difficulties involved. The Committee was particularly concerned that the presence of a tape recorder might inhibit suspects from giving information, that tapes could easily be tampered with and that unintelligible passages might give rise to lengthy wrangles at court over the admissibility of the record of the entire interrogation. It was also worried that if the use of tape recorders became standard, evidence of interrogations which were not recorded might be regarded as inferior and suspect. A minority of the Committee supported the compulsory use of tape recorders at police stations in the larger centres of population in order to reduce the incidence of confessions which are either secured through oppression or are fabricated or distorted. It felt that because the courts attach considerable importance to statements and evidence obtained during interrogation, it is crucial to ensure the validity of such statements.

Glanville Williams (1960) also writes in favour of tape recording; in common with the Criminal Law Revision Committee he recognises the possibility that tapes might be tampered with and to prevent this suggests that they be sealed by the accused person and deposited for transcription with an officer of the court. He also recognises police fears that a recording instrument would inhibit the answers of suspected persons, but suggests that if the procedure were recognised as standard practice, it would be unlikely to have too inhibiting an effect and would add greatly to the reliability of evidence.

In Australia, the Law Reform Commission (1975) also recommended tape recording. Its Report refers to the ease with which tape recorders can be used and their relative cheapness, and suggests that the full period of contact between police and suspect in serious cases could readily be taped, a procedure that is already used by the Victoria police in certain cases (para. 218). The Commission recommended various procedures to overcome the objections to tape recording that had been put to it. It suggested that inadmissible material on the tape could be edited out by a magistrate or lawyer unconnected with the case, after hearing submissions from both sides. Although the Commission recognised that electronic technology could detect whether or not tapes had been tampered with, the Report nevertheless recommends placing the tapes in safe custody and in the hands of persons other than the police (para. 158). Finally, the Report contains a detailed section on the legal arguments surrounding the use of monitoring devices.

Milte and Weber (1977) describe tape recording as the most efficient way of capturing a conversation, as well as the vocabulary and inflections of voice. They counter the legal objection that tape recorders 'constitute secondary evidence and are therefore not admissible under the best evidence rule' by reference to *R v Maqsud Ali*.[1] 'For many years now photographs have been admissible in evidence on proof that they are relevant to the issues involved in the case and that the prints are taken from negatives that are untouched . . . Evidence of things seen through telescopes or binoculars . . . has been admitted . . . We can see no difference in principle between a tape recording and a photograph . . .'

In 1976 the Home Office issued a Report on *The Feasibility of an Experiment in Tape-Recording Police Interrogations*. The Report concludes that a limited experiment, restricted to the tape recording of the taking of written statements would be technically feasible. The proposal has been criticised by several judicial and legal authorities as being too limited to be of value, and by police representatives as being too radical and difficult to implement (see, for example, the views of the Police Federation as reported in *The Times*, 20.10.1976).

Somewhat surprisingly, the Committee nowhere specifies the purpose of the tape recording. It would seem that its Report was prepared predominantly from the viewpoint of administrative convenience, rather than as a serious attempt to consider whether tape recording would be a feasible means of protecting the interests of suspects whilst at the same time assisting in law enforcement. Thus, it suggests only that written statements should be recorded, not the whole interrogation. Finally, the Committee makes great play of the dangers of tampering with tapes, and the administrative and financial problems associated with the need to provide transcripts, which it says will be required in a majority of cases — though it gives no reason for this assertion (para. 41). In the present writer's view it is extremely unlikely that transcripts would be required in any but a small minority of cases where some dispute arises. The fact that the interrogation has been recorded is likely to mean that the only accused to complain will be those who have strong evidence that what is said in court is incorrect; the tapes can then be produced to clarify the situation. The likelihood of frivolous complaints seems to be reduced, and the Committee's view that transcripts should be made automatically seems both expensive (as it points out) and to lack substantiation.

A study undertaken in the United States to establish the feasibility of video recording criminal investigations, including confessions, throws some light on these views (Gebhardt, 1975). Gebhardt writes that video tape is a valuable aid in the investigation of complex crime scenes. The test for admissibility of a tape is that it is relevant and material to the case and that it has been properly authenticated and verified. No transcripts are necessary and tapes are played back to the jury if required. Gebhardt claims that it is not expensive to have police vans equipped with video machinery, and no expertise is needed to operate it.

Apart from this feasibility study, two further instances of the use of recording equipment are worthy of note. A *World in Action* television programme entitled *Got it Taped* demonstrated dramatically how hidden

---

[1] [1965] 2 All E.R. 464 at 469.

cameras could be used to record and collect evidence during a criminal investigation.[1] The considerable advantages of video recording confessions were described by prosecutors and the police. Although confessions can be taped only with the suspect's agreement, it was nevertheless claimed that a substantial number of criminals had veen convicted on video evidence. One detective, who described conviction rates as 'astronomic', said he aimed at catching career criminals responsible for 150,000 offences every year. Although such figures must be viewed with caution, his explanation as to why so many convictions are obtained in this way is of particular interest. He argued that the jury are bewildered by the court set-up; in contrast, a television set (on which video recordings are played) is something they watch a great deal at home and understand: 'selling' a case to the jury is like selling a product on a commercial. The jury are able to see the defendant as he really is, not as he appears in court. Not surprisingly, a defence lawyer commented that the existence of a video confession has a very damaging effect on the preparation of the defence.

Further evidence of the usefulness of tape recorded interrogations and the problems associated with them comes from a study carried out by the Vera Institute of Justice in conjunction with the New York Police Department (Vera Institute of Justice, 1967). The study set out to record all interrogations following arrests for relatively serious crimes. It found that:

a. Of 275 tapes, 30 (11 per cent) had serious defects.
b. Sound recordings did not inhibit suspects from making statements. Of the 196 suspects who were told that they were to be recorded, only 4 (2 per cent) raised any question about it.
c. Several detectives felt that the tape recorder greatly inhibited their behaviour. They were more careful about the phrasing of questions and the 'sanitization' of their language.
d. During the 6 months of monitoring 41.1 per cent of all suspects interrogated made statements and of these, 57.6 per cent made admissions. These rates were no lower than those in the city's other 22 precincts. Three per cent of suspects admitted to offences other than that for which they had been arrested.
e. Despite written notices of monitoring sent to the Legal Aid Society (and, if relevant, to private counsel), not a single request was made to hear any tapes by a defendant's lawyer and in only one case did the prosecutor ask to hear the tape. No tapes were requested at trial.
f. On the question of 'voluntariness', listeners to the tapes were troubled by the fact that in 72 interrogations (26 per cent) they had serious doubts about the mental or physical state of the suspect. In a further 10 per cent of cases the suspect was an addict, had difficulty in expressing himself in English, or both. Whilst not in every such case was it clear that the defendant was not in a sufficiently stable frame of mind to comprehend

---

[1] This programme was shown on ATV in November 1977. The full story of the operation it described (known as the 'Washington Sting'), taken from the video tapes and voice recordings, as well as from interviews, official files, court records, trial testimony and exhibits, is to be found in Shaffer and Klose (1977).

what he was saying, the listeners felt that he may well have been incapable of protecting his own interests.

g. In all but 4 cases the *Miranda* warnings were given. However, the listeners expressed doubts about whether suspects understood the warnings; about the responses of the police to their questions and comments; about the speed with which a decision about a waiver was demanded; and about the initiation of a dialogue about the charge before the warnings were finally given. Finally, the listeners raised fundamental questions about the voluntariness of any waiver of the right to counsel when there was in fact, no counsel available, and about the efficacy of the suspects' right to terminate questioning once it had begun.

h. The time spent on interrogations was short. Ninety-five per cent of them took less than 20 minutes.

The authors draw attention to the fact that tape recording provides a far superior record of an interrogation than a dictated and signed confession and enables the listener to make his own judgment as to whether coercive tactics have been used by the police. They point out, however, that no sound recording can draw the distinction between legitimate questioning techniques and those which take unfair advantage of the suspect. The most frequently employed interrogation techniques were confronting the suspect with existing evidence, and pointing out inconsistencies in his story. Others, which occurred in a third of all interrogations were the open expression of scepticism about the suspect's story and stressing the complainant's viewpoint. In addition, suspects arrested together were frequently played off against each other. In some cases, suspects were accused of crimes other than the one for which they were arrested. Promises of intervention with the District Attorney, or similar incentives to cooperate, were occasionally used. In 11 per cent of cases, the combination of tactics appeared to the listeners to be sufficiently concentrated to constitute an 'aggressive' interrogation. These tended to be the longest interrogations.

Apart from the 72 cases mentioned above where the suspect's competence was in doubt, the authors say none of the statements made could be said to be involuntary. They add, 'the impression was almost universal that the interrogations were "cat and mouse affairs" and seldom did the suspect come off the better . . . Even in denying, most suspects gave away seemingly valuable leads'.

The exclusionary rule

In the United States the exclusionary rule prohibits the introduction of evidence which has been obtained by any form of improper police behaviour. Much of the extensive debate in that country over the exclusionary rule concerns its application to search and seizure.[1] In this country, debate has been much more limited and relates mainly to the voluntariness or otherwise of confessions.

---

[1] A discussion of the exclusionary rule as it relates to search and seizure is to be found in Spiotto, (1973) and *North Western University Law Review* (1975). See also Amsterdam (1974).

As was mentioned earlier, it is widely acknowledged that the judiciary do not effectively control the admission of evidence that has been obtained in contravention of the Judges' Rules. Glasbeek and Prentice (1968) refer to the fact that the failure of the courts to exercise their discretion to exclude evidence tempts the police 'whenever a suspect's guilt seems likely, to gamble that a violation of the Rules will not harm the chances of a conviction'. They add that 'the efficient operation of the Rules ultimately depends on the good will of specific law officers. At best this is a precarious safeguard' (p.483).

It would seem that English law does not see the problem of the admissibility of illegally obtained evidence in terms of individual rights and freedoms, but rather in terms of the relevance of the evidence. There appears to be a fear that the adoption of a general exclusionary rule would impede the operation of the criminal justice system.

Such an attitude seems strange in view of the fact that our near neighbours, the Scots, have gone some way to operating such a rule.[1] The recommendations put forward by Fisher in the *Confait* Report seem closer to Scottish practice. He proposes that 'it should be made a rule of law that no person should be convicted on the evidence of a confession obtained in any one of the following circumstances, *unless that evidence is supported by other evidence not obtained in any of such circumstances*' (his italics, para. 2.26). He lists four circumstances, one being 'a confession obtained in response to questioning by the police, by means of a breach of the Judges' Rules or Administrative Directions, whether or not the effect of the breach was to make the confession "involuntary" '.

As with the Judges' Rules generally, it is important to consider the *purpose* of the exclusionary rule. Three main justifications recur: that it eliminates prejudicial evidence; that it acts as a deterrent to unlawful conduct by the police; and that it preserves the integrity of the courts by preventing its involvement in illegal activity. Research in the United States has concluded that the exclusionary rule has failed to deter illegal conduct on the part of the police (Spiotto, 1973; Oaks, 1970). This has contributed to the considerable discussion over whether the rule ought not to be abandoned. Its supporters argue that to do so would '. . . not only accept governmental lawlessness, but also the implicit assumption that the only efficient form of law enforcement is lawless law enforcement. Such an assumption can only work to the detriment of the increasing professionalism of the police and further entrench those elements committed to the resistance of legal restrictions and court supervision . . . Whatever gains such a course may appear to hold on controlling crime, the ultimate effect is to disparage the rule of law on our society' (*North Western University Law Review,* 1975 p.798).

A further question which deserves attention is as follows: if the individual has indeed certain fundamental rights, including a right against self-incrimination has the state a duty to ensure that these rights be protected by law? Failure to do so may be said not only to make a mockery of the rights, but equally must erode public confidence in the administration of justice. On the other hand, in view of the practical necessities of law enforcement, the

---

[1] See, for example, Cross (1968), Gray (1966) and Heydon (1973).

question arises as to the extent to which the individual *should* be thus protected. Perhaps there will never be a clear solution to this dilemma; certainly the literature indicates that no country can claim to have resolved the problem surrounding the incompatibility between individual liberty and a degree of public safety.

Interrogation before a magistrate

A number of lawyers have put forward the suggestion that interrogation should only take place in the presence of an independent person; some claim that this can be a solicitor, but should not be the accused's counsel (Morton, 1972). Others insist that the independent party should be a magistrate (see, for example, *New Law Journal,* 1972; Justice, 1967; James, 1977), or some other independent judicial officer who could provide the necessary assurance that the suspect was not being subjected to pressures or unfair methods (Thompson, 1967). Thompson proposes that if the police are unduly hampered in their enquiries, a judicial officer should himself question the suspect and thus enable the trial court to draw appropriate inferences in cases of silence. Williams (1977) advocates a similar system, arguing that the continental system (he writes specifically about the French system) is fairer to the suspect since he is brought into (and protected by) the judicial situation at the earliest opportunity. Although Williams recognises that the practical working of the system may well depart from its theoretical principles, 'they are none the less sound for that'.

The Second Report of the Thomson Committee, *Criminal Procedure in Scotland* (1975) recommended that the prosecution or the accused should be allowed to ask for a judicial examination of the accused as soon as possible after arrest. This would enable the prosecution to ask questions so as to reduce the danger of subsequent fabrication of defences, and would permit enquiry as to whether the accused made the statements ascribed to him at the police station.

Not all share these views. The Criminal Law Revision Committee, for example, rejected interrogation before a magistrate on the grounds, *inter alia,* that the formality of the procedure would be likely to inhibit suspects from answering questions and that logistically it would be difficult to arrange. More important, however, the Committee thought that any such move would involve a departure from the present adversary system and its replacement by the continental European inquisitorial system.

Bowley (1975) considers that the continental system would be vastly more expensive to operate. Writing from the police perspective he argues that operational independence, which is seen as a safeguard against police subservience to the state, may be considerably modified.

The Law Reform Commission of Australia (1975) draws attention to the difficulty of finding people who would be available to corroborate every police investigation and suggests that the suspect's own lawyer, friend or relative would be a satisfactory substitute, though in serious cases an independent third person should be found. The Commission also draws attention to the need to offer some incentive to the police if such safeguards are to be used, and it suggests that a failure to use this (or any other means of corroboration) where it is practicable to do so, should *prima facie* result in the exclusion of the evidence (para 163).

The *Report of the Canadian Committee on Corrections* (1969) addresses similar issues. The Committee refers to the Justice proposal that a police officer should be empowered to take out a summons for the purpose of enabling him to interrogate the suspect before a magistrate but rejects such a system of compulsory interrogation (albeit with a legal representative present). It reports that police and law enforcement officers in Canada also rejected the proposal. The Committee points to the delay involved, and to the fact that professional criminals might use the procedure to get a fabricated defence on the record and avoid the rigorous cross-examination of crown counsel at the trial. Finally, it draws attention to the fact that the privilege against self-incrimination is deeply embedded in the feeling of justice and fairness which exists in contemporary Canadian society. *'We are of the opinion that such a long respected privilege should not be disturbed except for the clearest and most compelling reasons'* (authors' italics). This leads the Committee to conclude that interrogation before a judicial officer is neither necessary nor desirable, nor indeed would it increase the effectiveness of the present system of interrogation.

From a practical point of view, control of police activity is extremely problematic; as Amsterdam (1974) argues, the regulation of police practices involves a consideration of what *overall* powers the police should have and of the need to limit each power according to its nature, the interests of those it affects, and the abuses foreseeable in its exercise. 'But a very large part of the activities of the police are not specifically authorised by law; [they] are simply conducted by the police in the discharge of their broad general duties . . .' (p.386). The decisions as to where the lines are to be drawn should, ideally, reflect the perspectives of all citizens, but should recognise that these will almost certainly be competing if not conflicting perspectives. No amount of legal argument can resolve this dilemma – the issue is one of values.

CHAPTER 4

Some broader issues

'Truth' and 'facts'. How meaningful?

Much of the police literature discusses the importance of eliciting 'the truth', and the legal literature refers most often to 'the facts'. In an adversarial system of criminal justice, how meaningful are these terms?

Sir Robert Mark (1975) has argued that the establishment of 'truth' rather than the determination of technical 'guilt' should be the objective of the criminal justice system, and he believes the Judges' Rules prevent this insofar as they deflect from spontaneity and allow accused or suspected persons a period of reflection and consultation between arrest, interrogation and trial. This is a very different thing from saying that it is the policeman's duty to gather *evidence* and it is the duty of the court to determine *guilt*.

The criminal process is – at least theoretically – a device whereby issues of 'fact' can be litigated. But facts are not 'true' or 'false'; they either exist or they do not exist, and their determination can only be an issue of probability. Ideally, therefore, the rules of evidence and rights afforded to suspects in the pre-trial stage should not only protect the individual, but should contribute to the correct determination of these probabilities.

A proper development of this argument goes well beyond the terms of reference of this paper: it raises questions concerning not only the reliability of the evidence presented by the police and the 'voluntary' nature of any confession, but the reliability of other witnesses appearing in court.[1] Nevertheless, it is important that questions of this nature be borne in mind when considering the claims made by police and lawyers to the effect that the discovery of the facts, and hence the truth, underlies our criminal justice system.

The present survey of the literature has indicated that over the past twenty years very little has emerged concerning the *philosophy* (as distinct from the *technology*) of law enforcement that is new, let alone radical; the debates are very repetitive. In Australia, Canada and the United Kingdom, Commissions and Committees of Enquiry have been sifting through the same material for a very long time, and so the questions arise: why such weighty tomes, why such

---

[1] There is a substantial psychological literature dealing with this question and it is now well recognised that the testimony given in criminal trials is frequently unreliable. A review of the literature is given by Greer (1971).

expert evidence, and why so little change? One possible, and obviously only partial, explanation may lie in the extreme difficulty of reconciling legal thinking with sociological thinking; over time, changes in the law or in enforcement practices certainly occur, and they occur even in relation to the definition of the nature or seriousness of an act. But the legal mind is trained to look for 'objective truth' and 'objective facts' and to ignore the social nature of the law, and the relativity surrounding 'truth' and 'facts'. It is important to recognise that there are various, and often competing definitions of reality, and these social definitions are *imposed* upon 'facts'. Such fundamental sociological concepts[1] need to be appreciated and understood by the legal community and must be made relevant to legal argument if major changes are to emerge from the work of the Commissions and Committees of Enquiry.

The limits of authority. What kind of police? What kind of powers? The need for a sociological perspective

One of the major issues to emerge from this paper, no matter what aspect of pre-trial investigation is being discussed, is the conflict between what the police believe is expected of their law enforcement role (which in essence reflects, and is a reflection of, their own perception of their role), and the rights of the individual, insofar as these reflect a society holding democratic values and with a sense of justice and fairness. The conflict is becoming more, rather than less acute, and as Lewis (1976) and others point out, the growth of serious crime, the increasing use of terrorist techniques, internal militancy within the police over pay and conditions and growing industrial unrest have all brought home to the public, as well as to the police, the need to reconsider the role of the police.[2] Any detailed discussion of these issues falls outside the scope of this report, but crime detection and criminal investigation have to be included in that future role and the organisation of the force plays an important part in determining how these aspects of policing will be carried out.

Of equal, if not greater importance, however, is the extent to which the societal changes mentioned above bring about new or different public expectations of the police role. For example, many people (perhaps the majority) expect the police to 'get tough' in situations of urban unrest, demonstrations, etc and it would be unrealistic to suppose that the approach and behaviour of the police will differ as between these situations and their other law enforcement activities. This means that a substantial sector of the public will be legitimising a 'law and order' model of policing, yet there is at the same time an implicit assumption that the law could actually be made to work as it is supposed to, fairly and impartially in the interests of all. This issue is well covered by Chambliss and Seidman (1971). A similar point is made by Johnson and Gregory (1971): 'The means required to achieve police ends may often conflict with the conduct required of the police as legal actors.

---

[1] For a discussion of these concepts see Berger and Luckmann (1967).
[2] See on this 'What kind of Police?' *New Society*, 25.8.1977.

There are those who believe that police should have more power and more freedom in terms of the law. On the other hand there are those who emphasise that police must stick to the Rule of Law.'

As will have been apparent from the review of the literature thus far, the debate about police freedom, as exemplified by reference to the Judges' Rules, has been largely legal, philosophical or plainly emotional; very little attention has been paid to the sociological pressures which lead to abuses of police powers. Yet these are clearly demonstrated in both this country by Cain (1973) and in the United States by Rubenstein (1973). Their studies imply that if the organisation and administration of police work continues to develop along present lines, it is to be expected that police malpractice together with police-initiated demands for greater freedom and immunity from public scrutiny will be likely to increase. Both these books were published in 1973 (and are based upon field work carried out earlier), and the intervening years have demonstrated how correct are the implications which the authors drew from their findings.

Similar sociological points are also made by Blumberg (1970) who details a number of organisational factors which tend to deflect the police from complying with the demands of due process. *Inter alia*, he refers to the fact that it is occupational and career commitments that are responsible for law enforcement priorities, rather than the stated organisational goals of due process and the rule of law. He notes that secrecy and relative immunity from scrutiny enable the police in the United States to adopt institutionalised evasions of due process requirements. These observations are also relevant to this country.

If changes in police practice are thought to be desirable, it will be crucial that the police accept such changes as legitimate. They are more likely to do so if we first have a better understanding of how they perceive their role, and an analysis of the organisational influences that critically affect their approach to crime and criminals. Finally, it is legitimate to ask a very important question: to what extent *can* the present criminal process be modified to meet the conflicting demands currently made of it? As Hogarth (1973) has observed, 'adversarial proceedings, with their concentration on due process, all or nothing outcomes, and formally defined rights and wrongs, lack the capacity to reconcile differences that exist between individuals or between individuals and the group . . . Stepping up the war against crime will provide employment in the anti-crime industry, but will do little to solve the underlying problems that exist in society' (p.3).

Bibliography

Amsterdam, A. 1974 Perspective on the fourth amendment. *Minnesota Law Rev.,* 58, 349 – 477.

Arens, R. and Meadow, A. 1956 Psycholinguistics and the confession dilemma. *Columbia Law Rev.,* 56, 19 – 46.

Ashworth, A. J. 1976 Some blueprints for criminal investigation. *Crim. Law Rev.,* 594 – 609.

Baldwin, J. and McConville, M. 1977 *Negotiated Justice.* Martin Robertson, London.

Bator, B. and Vorenberg, J. 1976 Arrest, detention, interrogation and the right to counsel. *Columbia Law Rev.,* 66, 62.

Berger. P and Luckmann, T. 1967 *The Social Construction of Reality.* Doubleday Anchor, New York.

Bittner, E. 1974 Florence Nightingale in pursuit of Willie Sutton: a theory of the police, in Jacob, H. (ed) 1974 *The Potential for Reform of Criminal Justice.* Sage Publications, Beverly Hills.

Bittner, E. 1975 *The Functions of the Police in Modern Society.* Aronson.

Blumberg, A. 1970 *Criminal Justice.* 2nd Ed., Quadrangle Books, Chicago.

Bottomley, A. K. and Coleman, C. 1976 Criminal statistics: the police role in the discovery and detection of crime. *Int. Jnl. of Crim. and Pen.,* 4, 33 – 58.

Bottoms, A. and McClean, J. 1975 *Defendants in the Criminal Process.* Routledge and Kegan Paul, London.

Bowley, A. S. 1975 Prosecution – a matter for the police. *Crim. Law Rev.,* 442 – 43.

Bredemeir, H. C. 1977 Survey of literature on social excahnge theory. *Contemporary Sociology,* 6, 646 – 650.

Cain, M. 1971 On the beat: interactions and relations in urban and rural police forces, in Cohen, S. (ed) 1971 *Images of Deviance.* Penguin Books, Harmondsworth.

Cain, M. 1973 *Society and the Policeman's Role.* Routledge and Kegan Paul, London.

Chambliss, W. and Seidman, R. 1971 *Law, Order and Power.* Addison-Wesley, Reading, Mass.

Chatterton, M. 1976a Police in social control, in *Control without Custody.* Cropwood Papers, 1976, Institute of Criminology, University of Cambridge.

Chatterton, M. 1976b The social contexts of violence, in Borland, M. (ed) 1976 *Violence and the Family.* Manchester University Press.

Cox, B., Shirley, J. and Short, M. 1977 *The Fall of Scotland Yard.* Penguin Books, Harmondsworth.

Criminal Law Review 1967 Questioning: a comment, by a Barrister, 91 – 94.

Criminal Law Review 1971 Right to Silence, 501 – 502.

Criminal Law Revision Committee 1972 *Eleventh Report: Evidence (General).* Cmnd. 4991. HMSO, London.

Cronkhite, Clyde L. 1974 *Automation and Law Enforcement.* Chas. C. Thomas, Springfield, Ill.

Cross, R. 1968 *Evidence.* 3rd Ed., Butterworths, London.

Crowley, W. D. 1973 The interrogation of suspects. *Int. Crim. Pol. Rev.,* 28, 203 – 210.

Deeley, P. 1971 *Beyond Breaking Point: A Study of Techniques of Interrogation.* Arthur Barker Ltd., London.

Devlin, P. 1960 *The Criminal Prosecution in England.* Oxford University Press.

Driver, E. 1968 Confessions and the social psychology of coercion. *Harvard Law Rev.,* 82, 42 – 61.

Firth, A. 1975 Interrogation. *Police Review,* No. 4324, 1507.

Franklin, C. 1970 *The Third Degree.* Robert Hale, London.

Gebhardt, R. H. 1975 Video tape in criminal cases. *FBI Law Enforcement Bulletin,* May, 6 – 10.

Glasbeek, H. and Prentice, D. 1968 The criminal suspect's illusory right of silence in the British Commonwealth. *Cornell Law Quarterly,* 53, 473.

Goldstein, H. 1963 Police discretion: The ideal versus the real. *Public Admin. Rev.,* 23, 140 – 148.

Goodsall, J. E. 1974 The professional interviewer. *Police Review,* No. 4241, 525.

Gordon, F. A. 1964 Interrogation. *New Zealand Police Journal,* Feb/March.

Gray, J. 1966 The admissibility of evidence illegally or unfairly obtained in Scotland. *Jurid. Rev.,* 11, 89 – 114.

Greer, D. S. 1971 Anything but the truth? The reliability of testimony in criminal trials. *Brit. Jnl. Criminol.,* 11, 131 – 154.

Greenawalt, K. 1974 Perspectives on the right to silence, in Hood, R. (ed) 1974 *Crime, Criminology and Public Policy.* Heinemann, London.

Griffith, J. 1977 *The Politics of the Judiciary.* Fontana.

Griffiths, J. and Ayres, R. E. 1976 A postscript to the *Miranda* project: interrogation of draft protesters. *Yale Law Jnl.,* 77, 318.

Hartjen, C. 1972 Police-citizen encounters: social order in interpersonal interaction. *Criminology,* 10, 61 – 84.

Heydon, J. D. 1973 Illegally obtained evidence. *Crim. Law Rev.,* 603 – 12 and 690 – 99.

Home Office 1964 *Judges' Rules and Administrative Directions to the Police.* Circular No. 31/1964. HMSO, London.

Home Office 1976 *The Feasibility of an Experiment in the Tape-recording of Police Interrogations.* Cmnd. 6630. HMSO, London.

Home Office 1978 *Judges' Rules and Adminstrative Directions to the Police.* Circular No. 89/1978. HMSO, London.

Hogarth, J. 1973 *Alternatives to the Adversary System*. Unpublished MS. Vancouver, B.C.

Inbau, F. E. 1961 Police interrogation – a practical necessity. *Jnl. Crim. Law, Criminol. and Pol. Sci.*, 52, 16 – 20.

Inbau, F. E. and Reid, J. 1967 *Criminal Interrogation and Confessions*. 2nd Ed., Williams & Wilkins, Baltimore.

James, L. 1977 Assisting the police with their enquiries. *Justice of the Peace*, 141, 307 – 310.

Johnson, D. and Gregory, R. 1971 Police-community relations in the United States: a review of recent literature and projects. *Jnl. Crim. Law, Criminol. and Pol. Sci.*, 62, 94 – 103.

Justice, 1967 Evidence Committee. *The Interrogation of Suspects*. London.

Keeton, G. 1977 The Judges' Rules. *Justice of the Peace*, 141, 516 – 518.

Kuh, R. H. 1966 The 'rest of us' in the 'policing the police' controversy. *Jnl. Crim. Law, Criminol and Pol. Sci.*, 57, 244 – 250.

LaFave, W. R. 1965 *Arrest: The Decision to Take a Suspect into Custody*. Little, Brown & Co., Boston.

Lambert, J. R. 1970 *Crime, Police and Race Relations*. Oxford University Press.

Lanham, O. 1974 Arrest, detention and compulsion. *Crim. Law Rev.*, 288 – 297.

Laurie, P. 1970 *Scotland Yard*. Bodley Head.

Law Reform Commission of Australia 1975 *Criminal Investigation*. Report No. 2. Australian Govt. Publishing Service, Canberra.

Leigh, L. H. 1975 *Police Powers in England and Wales*. Butterworths, London.

Leiken, L. S. 1970 Police interrogation in Colorado: the implementation of *Miranda*. *Denver Law Jnl.*, 47, 1 – 53.

Lewis, R. 1976 *A Force for the Future: the Role of the Police in the Next Ten Years*. Temple-Smith, London.

Lewis, P. and Allen, H. 1977 Participating *Miranda*: an attempt to subvert certain constitutional safeguards. *Crime and Delinquency*, 23, 75 – 80.

Lidstone, K. 1977 *Arresting thoughts*. Unpublished MS.

Mark, R. 1972 *The Disease of Crime: Punishment or Treatment?* Lecture given to the Royal Society of Medicine, June 1972. William Clowes and Sons, London.

Mark, R. 1975 Truth, not guilt is the question that matters. *Police*, VIII, 16 – 17.

Martin, J. and Wilson, G. 1969 *The Police: a Study in Manpower*. Heinemann, London.

Marx, E. 1952 Psychosomatics and coerced confessions. *Dickinson Law Rev.*, 57, 1 – 23.

McCabe, S. and Purves, R. 1972a *The Jury at Work*. Basil Blackwell, Oxford.

McCabe, S. and Purves, R. 1972b *By-passing the Jury*. Basil Blackwell, Oxford.

Medalie, R., Zeitz, L. and Alexander, P. 1968 Custodial police interrogation in our nation's capital: an attempt to implement *Miranda*. *Michigan Law Rev.*, 66, 1347 – 1421.

Mettler, G. B. 1977 *Criminal Investigation*. Holbrook Press.

Miller, C. J. 1973 Silence and confessions: what are they worth? *Crim. Law Rev.,* 343 – 355.

Miller, W. 1977 *Cops and Bobbies: Police Authority in New York and London 1830 – 1870.* Univ. of Chicago Press.

Milte, K. L. and Weber, T. 1977 *Police in Australia: Development, Functions and Procedures.* Butterworths, Sydney.

Monkkonen, E. H. 1977 Review of Miller, W. 'Cops and Bobbies' in *Contemporary Sociology,* 6, 552.

Morton, J. 1972 The rights of suspects. *New Law Jnl.,* 122, 805 – 806.

Morton, J. 1975 To Combat Verbals. *New Law Jnl.,* 125, 830 – 1.

National Advisory Commission on Criminal Justice Standards and Goals 1973 *Task Force on the Police*. US Govt. Printing Office, Washington, DC.

Neubauer, D. W. 1974 Confessions in Prairie City: some causes and effects. *Jnl. Crim. Law & Criminol.,* 65, 103 – 112.

New Law Journal 1972 Rules of the criminal process, 122, 573 – 74.

New Society 1977 What kind of Police?, 41, 378.

Neiderhoffer, A. 1967 *Behind the Shield: the Police in Urban Society.* Doubleday, New York.

North Western University Law Review 1975 Critique: on the limitations of empirical evaluations of the exclusionary rule: a critique of the Spiotto Research in *US v Calandra*. 69, 740 – 778.

Oaks, D. 1970 Studying the exclusionary rule in search and seizure. *Univ. of Chicago Law Rev.,* 37, 665.

O'Hara, C. 1973 *Fundamentals of Criminal Investigation.* 3rd Ed., Chas. C. Thomas, Springfield, Ill.

Pepinsky, H. 1970 A theory of police reaction to *Miranda v Arizona. Crime and Delinquency,* 16, 379 – 392.

Pogrebin, M. 1976 Some observations on the detective role. *Jnl. of Pol. Sci. and Admin.,* 4, 277 – 284.

President's Commission on Law Enforcement and the Administration of Justice 1967 *Task Force Report: the Police.* US Govt. Printing Office, Washington, DC.

Reik, T. 1959 *The Compulsion to Confess: On the Psychoanalysis of Crime and Punishment.* Farrar, Straus and Cudahy, New York.

Reiser, M. 1973 *Practical Psychology for Police Officers.* Chas. C. Thomas, Springfield, Ill.

Reiss, A. J. 1971 *The Police and the Public.* Yale University Press, New Haven.

Reiss, A. J. and Bordua, D. J. 1966 Environment and organisation: a perspective on the police, in Bordua, D. J. (ed) 1966 *The Police: Six Sociological Essays.* Wiley, New York.

Report of an Inquiry by the Hon. Sir Henry Fisher into the circumstances leading to the trial of three persons on charges arising out of the death of Maxwell Confait and the fire at 27 Doggett Road, London SE6. 1977 HMSO, London.

Report of the Canadian Committee on Corrections, Toward Unity: Criminal Justice and Corrections. 1969 Queen's Printer, Ottawa.

The Right to Silence: Symposium 1973 Proceedings of the Institute of Criminology, University of Sydney, No. 17.

The Royal Commission into Metropolitan Toronto Police Practices 1976. Queen's Printer, Ontario.

Royal, R. F. and Schutt, S. 1976 *Gentle Art of Interviewing and Interrogation: A Professional Manual and Guide.* Prentice-Hall, Englewood Cliffs, New Jersey.

Rubenstein, J. 1973 *City Police.* Farrar, Straus and Giroux, New York.

Scottish Home and Health Department and Crown Office 1975 *Criminal Procedure in Scotland (Second Report).* Cmnd. 6218. HMSO, Edinburgh.

Seeburger, R. H. and Wettick, R. S. 1967 *Miranda* in Pittsburgh: a statistical study. *Univ. of Pittsburgh Law Rev.,* 29, 1 – 26.

Shearing, C. and Leon, J. 1977 Reconsidering the police role: a challenge to a challenge of a popular conception. *Canadian Jnl. of Crim. and Corrections,* 19, 331 – 345.

Sheley, J. and Harris, A. 1976 Communication: on police-citizen encounters. *Social Problems,* 23, 630 – 631.

Schaffer, R. and Klose, K. 1977 *Surprise! Surprise! How the Lawmen Conned the Thieves.* Viking Press.

Skolnick, J. H. 1966 *Justice Without Trial: Law Enforcement in a Democratic Society.* Wiley, New York.

Sobel, N. R. 1966 *The New Confession Standards.* Gould Publications, New York.

Spiotto, J. E. 1973 Search and seizure: an empirical study of the exclusionary rule and its alternative. *Jnl. of Legal Studies,* 2, 243 – 278.

Steer, D. 1970 *Police Cautions: A Study in the Exercise of Police Discretion.* Basil Blackwell, Oxford.

Stinchcombe, A. L. 1968 *Constructing Social Theories.* Harcourt, Brace and World Inc., New York.

Sykes, R. and Clark, J. 1975 A theory of deference exchange in police-civilian encounters. *Amer. Jnl. Sociol.,* 81, 584 – 600.

The Task Force on Policing in Ontario 1974 *Report to the Solicitor General,* Queen's Printer, Toronto.

Thomas, D. A. 1964 The revised Judge's Rules. *Brit. Jnl. Criminol.,* 4, 383 – 385.

Thompson, D. 1967 Questioning: a comment. *Crim. Law Rev.,* 94 – 100.

Tifft, L. L. 1975 Control systems, social bases of power and power exercise in police organisations. *Jnl. Pol. Sci. and Admin.,* 3, 66 – 76.

The Times 1968 Discrediting the police. 9 September 1968.

Van Meter, C. H. 1973 *Principles of Police Interrogation.* Chas. C. Thomas, Springfield, Ill.

Vera Institute of Justice 1967 *Taping Police Interrogations in the 20th Precinct NYPD.* Unpublished MS.

Wald, M., Ayres, R., Hess, D. W., Schantz, M. and Whitebread, C. H. 1967 Interrogations in New Haven: the impact of *Miranda. Yale Law Jnl.,* 76, 1519 – 1648.

Wegg-Prosser, C. 1973 *The Police and the Law.* Oyez, London.

Weisberg, B. 1961 Police interrogation of arrested persons: a skeptical view. *Jnl. Crim. Law, Criminol. and Pol. Sci.,* 52, 21 – 46.

Westley, W. 1970 *The Police: A Study of Law, Custom and Morality*. MIT Press, Cambridge, Mass.

Wicks, R. J. 1974 *Applied Psychology for Law Enforcement and Correction Officers*. McGraw Hill.

Wilcox, A. F. 1972 *The Decision to Prosecute*. Butterworths, London.

Wiley, M. G. and Hudik, T. 1974 Police-citizen encounters: a field test of exchange theory. *Social Problems,* 22, 119 – 127.

Williams, D. 1977 Investigation: why we should follow the French tradition? *Police Review,* No. 4395, 446 – 7.

Williams, G. 1960 Questioning by the police: some practical considerations. *Crim. Law Rev.,* 325 – 346.

Williams, G. 1961 Police interrogation privileges and limitations under foreign law: England. *Jnl. Crim. Law, Criminol. and Pol. Sci.,* 52, 50 – 57.

Williams, G. 1963 *The Proof of Guilt*. 3rd Ed., Stevens & Sons, London.

Wilson, J. Q. 1968 *Varieties of Police Behaviour*. Harvard University Press, Cambridge, Mass.

Wilson, O. W. 1977 *Police Planning* 2nd Ed., Chas. C. Thomas, Springfield, Ill.

Witt, J. W. 1973 Non-coercive interrogation and the administration of criminal justice: the impact of *Miranda* on police effectuality. *Jnl. Crim. Law and Criminol.,* 64, 320 – 332.

Zander, M. 1972a Access to a solicitor in the police station. *Crim. Law Rev.,* 342 – 350.

Zander, M. 1972b Informing the suspect of his right in the police station. *Law Soc. Gazette,* 69, 1238.

Zander, M. 1977a The criminal process – a subject ripe for a major inquiry. *Crim. Law Rev.,* 249 – 58.

Zander, M. 1977b When is an arrest not an arrest? *New Law Jnl.,* 127, 352 – 54.

Zimbardo, P. 1967 The psychology of police confessions. *Psychology Today,* June, 17 – 20 and 25 – 27.

Police Interrogation:
An Observational Study in Four Police Stations

Paul Softley

with the assistance of David Brown,
Bob Forde, George Mair and David Moxon

Acknowledgements

I should like to thank the police forces which co-operated in this study and in particular police liaison officers and other senior officers at the police stations visited.

Several colleagues assisted in the research: John Ditchfield played a part in developing the study; and in particular David Moxon, George Mair and David Brown were involved in preparation of the final drafts.

Paul Softley

Home Office Research Unit
December 1979

Contents

List of Tables

CHAPTER 1

Introduction

Police interrogation, or the questioning of suspects in the custody of the police, plays a vital part in bringing offenders to justice and is now an established feature of the criminal process in England and Wales. It has also become the most controversial feature of the whole criminal process since the publication, in 1972, of the Criminal Law Revision Committee's report on evidence,[1] the reaction to which has highlighted an unresolved clash of opinion between those who believe that the powers of the police to question suspects should be enlarged and those who believe that such powers should, in effect, be curbed. How those powers are used forms the subject of the research described in this report.

The study, initially modelled on an American research project on the implementation and effect of the Supreme Court decision in *Miranda v Arizona*,[2] (Wald *et al*, 1967), focused on interviews with suspects and employed the method of direct observation. It did not rely on official records, or the recollections of prisoners or police officers, though reference was made to station records and the opportunity was taken of discussing cases with the officers involved. The object was to provide an account of what happens to a prisoner or suspect from the time he arrives at the police station until he is released or put into a cell after being charged. More specifically the aims of the study were:

a. to examine the operation of the Judges' Rules and Administrative Directions to the Police, and

b. to assess the contribution of questioning to the detection of crime.

Sample and methods

The study was undertaken in four police stations, one each in West Yorkshire, Nottinghamshire, Avon and Somerset and the Metropolitan Police District. In order to ensure that a sufficiently large sample was obtained within the time available, each of the stations was a busy town centre one. Consequently thefts from stores were more common and burglaries from dwellings were less

---

[1] Criminal Law Revision Committee, *Eleventh Report, Evidence (General)*.

[2] See above, p.4 fn.

common than would have been expected with a more varied selection of stations. The study had the full support of chief officers and the research proceeded on the basis of full consultation. The points were stressed that the project was not a formal investigation, or a check to see whether policemen were complying with force orders; that individual officers would not be named in any report; that the observer would merely observe and would not take contemporaneous notes in an interview, unless the investigating officer was taking notes, and that the observer would retire at the request of the investigating officer.

Between 1 February 1979 and 1 May 1979, a team from the Home Office Research Unit made two visits of six days to each provincial force area and one visit of four days to the Metropolitan Police District. During each period of attachment, the team aimed at 24 hour coverage and operated a system of three 8 hour shifts, similar to that worked by the police themselves.

The observers concentrated on criminal cases. Motorists brought to the police station for routine tests, prostitutes and drunkards were excluded from the sample, as were persons surrendering to police bail and persons, arrested on a warrant, who were not wanted for questioning. Details of the cases observed were recorded on forms, each relating to one prisoner or suspect. The purpose of the form was to standardise observation; but this did not preclude observers from taking notes on any occurrence that struck them as interesting and pertinent.

Usually only one member of the research team was on duty at any one time. In three out of the four stations, the observer was situated in or close to the charge room, when not otherwise engaged, so that he could see suspects being brought in and could take up a case immediately the suspect arrived, without having to rely on the police to notify him, but in the fourth he had to rely largely on the police to notify him. In the interview, the police and suspect usually sat at a table, and the observer generally sat to one side. The observer was ignored by the police unless the suspect questioned his presence or the police felt that it was desirable to introduce him.

Because it was impracticable for observers to follow through every case, they tended to concentrate on the more serious ones. The final sample consisted of 218 prisoners or suspects, 61 per cent of the 359 persons who were eligible for inclusion. As Table 1:1 shows, observers gave priority to offences of burglary, wounding or assault occasioning actual bodily harm, and deception. Minor assaults and thefts from stores were under-represented. So too, by chance, was handling.

Not all interviews could be observed. Of a total of 245 interviews, 18 (7 per cent) were partly or entirely missed because the observer was working elsewhere, five were missed because the suspect objected to the observer's presence, and two were partly missed because the investigating officer wanted a word in private with the suspect.

More than 60 suspects were observed at each of the provincial police stations and 30 were observed in London. Four-fifths (81 per cent) were males. Almost a quarter (23 per cent) were juveniles, and only one-fifth (21 per cent) were over 30. Ninety per cent were white skinned and 7 per cent were negroid. Only 42 per cent were in paid employment, most of them in skilled manual

Table 1:1 Coverage of suspects during periods of observation: an analysis by offence

Offence	Suspects observed	Suspects not observed	Total
	%	%	% (N)
Burglary	95.8	4.2	100.0 (24)
Theft from store	49.3	50.7	100.0 (134)
Other theft	59.3	40.7	100.0 (54)
Handling	14.3	85.7	100.0 (7)
Unauthorised taking of motor vehicle	69.6	30.4	100.0 (23)
Deception	85.7	14.3	100.0 (14)
Wounding or assault occasioning actual bodily harm	81.1	18.9	100.0 (37)
Minor assault	42.4	57.6	100.0 (33)
Criminal damage	76.5	23.5	100.0 (17)
Other	68.7	31.3	100.0 (16)
Total	*60.7*	*39.3*	*100.0 (359)*

occupations. Twenty per cent were at school or college; 6 per cent were housewives or retired persons, and 28 per cent might be described as unemployed, seeking work. (Employment status was not ascertained for the remaining 4 per cent of suspects.) Over one half of the adult suspects had a criminal record and almost one half (42 per cent) of the juveniles had been in trouble before.

The principal offence of which persons were suspected is shown in Table 1:2. In this table, as in Table 1:1, the other offences referred to include possession of drugs, sexual offences (indecent assault and unlawful sexual intercourse), possession of an offensive weapon and robbery. Twenty four suspects (11 per cent) were involved in what police officers described as serious crime. This included several burglaries and cheque frauds, theft, handling and

Table 1:2 Offences of which observed persons were suspected.

Offence	Suspects	
	No.	%
Burglary	23	10.6
Theft from store	66	30.3
Other theft	32	14.7
Handling	1	0.4
Unauthorised taking of a motor vehicle	16	7.3
Deception	12	5.5
Wounding or assault occasioning actual bodily harm	30	13.8
Minor assault	14	6.4
Criminal damage	13	6.0
Other	11	5.0
Total	*218*	*100.0*

wounding. Perhaps the most serious case seen by the research team was a burglary in which equipment with a retail value of several thousand pounds was stolen.

Juveniles tended to be involved in less serious offences than adults. Only one was suspected of burglary; three were suspected of wounding or assault occasioning actual bodily harm, and 27 (54 per cent) were suspected of theft from stores.

Some limitations of the study

Before considering the results of the study, it is important to recognise its shortcomings.

First, the sample cannot be said to be representative of the country or even of the police forces in which it took place. The research was an observational study of just four police stations, and at one of these, in the Metropolitan Police District, the actual period of attachment was much less than the research team had planned.

Second, the presence of observers will inevitably have had some effect on the police. The nature of this effect is hard to assess. Observers felt that a number of officers, particularly some of the younger and less experienced ones, may have been apprehensive about their presence and made a special point of adhering to the procedures laid down. Other officers may have been stimulated to show off their skills in questioning by displaying a rather wider range of techniques and tactics than a particular case might otherwise have warranted. Observers did not gain the impression, from their many informal contacts with officers, that their presence had led to marked changes in the normal pattern of police practices – a typical remark was that the officer quickly forgot the observer as he became involved in the task in hand.

There is no way, however, short of extended participant observation in all the forces concerned, of judging to what extent the observer became, as one officer said he did after a couple of minutes, part of the furniture. General social research experience suggests that it takes time to build up the personal familiarity and relationship of trust that are necessary for an observer to become an entirely neutral factor in the behaviour of the observed. Where the observed, as in this case, constitute an occupational group which is frequently under attack for its real or imagined behaviour, it is to be expected that the effects of observer presence are likely to be slow to disappear. Relations in this study between observers and police were amicable, and the fact that observers saw themselves not as scrutinising or critically inspecting police practices, but as concerned faithfully to describe the realities and problems, may have done much to allay suspicion. Nonetheless, observers would not claim that they had, by the end of their period of observations, become so familiar to police as to be indistinguishable from police colleagues.

In view of the concern that has sometimes been publicly expressed about police interrogation practices, the problem of observer effect is most critical in relation to the question of possible serious breaches of the Judges' Rules. It seems realistic to acknowledge that, following the thorough preliminary briefing given to police, observers would have been unlikely to see any behaviour which was in flagrant breach of the Rules. None, certainly, was observed. But it might also be reasonable to expect that any routine practices which might periodically involve relatively minor breaches of the Rules would be more likely to emerge because it would be more trouble to change them and less worth the effort to do so. If such minor breaches were widespread and apparently endemic, there might be grounds for suspecting the possibility of more serious breaches. Although minor breaches were observed, they did not appear to observers to amount to systematic disregard of the Rules. The authors feel confident in asserting, although they cannot prove it, that the general picture they formed of police questioning and the operation of the Judges' Rules at the four stations where observations took place was, for the most part, a reliable one.

Third, the team did not, with one or two possible exceptions, observe interrogation of any suspect held in connection with the most serious types of crime. There were, for example, no cases of murder, armed robbery or rape. It is perhaps in relation to such crimes that the pressures on police to bring offenders to justice are normally strongest. In consequence it may be here that the Judges' Rules put special strains on questioning. On the other hand, it may be that the gravity of such crimes would encourage rigid adherence to the letter of the Rules. It was made clear to the Home Office Research Unit by some senior police officers, when the study was being set up, that they would not wish independent observers to be present at such interrogations, not out of concern over possible police improprieties, but out of regard for the particularly sensitive nature of the offences. This study can say nothing about interrogation in connection with the most serious crimes; but it should be noted that, in cases where allegations have been made of major breaches of the Judges' Rules, some of which have been substantiated, it has not always been serious crimes that have been under investigation.

CHAPTER 2

Arrival at the police station and time spent there

At the police station, the quietest time is between 6am and 9am, when the night shift finishes and the officers on early turn report for duty. The CID will interview some of the suspects brought in overnight before they are bailed or taken to court. Later, a few new suspects will be brought in, as a result of enquiries or fresh offences such as shoplifting; but the period between 9am and midday is not much busier than the period between 3am and 6am. The busiest times can never be predicted with certainty, but they tend to be the late afternoon and early evening, when the trickle of shoplifters is swollen by school children; the period between 10pm and midnight, when the pubs, cinemas and restaurants close; and the early hours of the morning when the clubs close and the last of the revellers leave the town centre deserted until it fills with shop and office workers in the morning rush hour. Petty crime is largely a leisure time pursuit.

Table 2:1 shows, in relation to the nature of the offence, the times at which suspects arrived at the police station.

Table 2:1 Time of arrival by offence

Time of Arrival	Burglary	Theft from store	Other theft	Wounding or assault	Other	Total
	Suspects %	Suspects %	Suspects %	Suspects %	Suspects %	Suspects %
0601 – 0900	0.0	0.0	0.0	2.3	1.9	0.9
0901 – 1200	8.7	12.1	9.4	6.8	0.0	7.3
1201 – 1500	4.3	31.8	12.5	6.8	9.4	15.6
1501 – 1800	8.7	56.1	18.7	6.8	18.9	26.6
1801 – 2100	26.1	0.0	21.9	13.6	1.9	9.2
2101 – 2359	26.1	0.0	15.6	40.9	20.8	18.3
0001 – 0300	17.4	0.0	15.6	20.5	39.6	17.9
0301 – 0600	8.7	0.0	6.3	2.3	7.5	4.1
Total	*100.0*	*100.0*	*100.0*	*100.0*	*100.0*	*100.0*
	(N = 23)	(N = 66)	(N = 32)	(N = 44)	(N = 53)	(N = 218)

Seventy per cent of persons suspected of burglary arrived at the police station between 6pm and 3am – the pattern would presumably be somewhat different in the summer months when the evenings are lighter – and over half the persons arrested for theft from a store arrived between 3pm and 6pm.

Other thefts were, not unexpectedly, more evenly distributed throughout the day. Over 60 per cent of persons who were at the police station in connection with a wounding, an assault, or other offence arrived between 9pm and 3am.

The vast majority (97 per cent) of the 218 suspects observed by the research team were under arrest: only 6 were not arrested. Two hundred and four (94 per cent) were arrested prior to arrival at the police station, and 8 were arrested on arrival. Police officers rarely invited suspects to the station for interview, though the practice appeared to be more common in some forces than in others. Most of the suspects who went voluntarily to the police station did so because they knew, or believed, that they were wanted for questioning, but two or three turned themselves in because they were troubled by a bad conscience. One such person brought with her a ring that she had stolen. On being asked whether she had committed other offences, she confessed to stealing a bottle of perfume. 'But', she added, 'I can't give that back. It had such a beautiful scent I used it all.'

Persons who were taken to the police station as suspects generally arrived there shortly after being arrested. Over four fifths arrived within 20 minutes of the time of arrest, and slightly less than one tenth arrived after 30 minutes. Five suspects arrived at the police station over an hour after they had been arrested.

Observers enquired of case officers the nature and source of the information which resulted in a suspect being arrested, or invited to attend the station for interview. In one half of the cases the information came from the victim or loser (or a store detective employed by the loser); in one fifth it came from some other law-abiding member of the public, such as a neighbour or passer-by, and in a similar proportion of cases the source of information was a police officer. The information against 6 per cent of suspects was given by another suspect or an informer, and for slightly less than 2 per cent of suspects the initial information was given by the suspect himself, who was worried by some transgression.

For each of the main types of offence under investigation an attempt was made to categorise the nature of the information against the suspect. The results are shown in Tables A:1 to A:5 in the Appendix. In the majority of cases there was strong evidence linking the suspect to the offence: two thirds of suspects were either caught in the act, observed or detained at the scene of the crime, or found in possession of stolen property. In other cases the evidence, though often strong, was usually circumstantial. The suspect might have been seen in the company of another suspect, or with a group involved in an offence, or he may have been observed near the scene of a crime in circumstances which pointed to his involvement. Occasionally a suspect was brought in as a result of information from a police informer or a suspect already under arrest. In most cases, even where the evidence was strong, further investigation was necessary before the police could decide whether to prosecute, caution, or release the suspect.

What happens to a suspect when he is arrested and taken to a police station will to some extent depend on the facilities of the station, the practice of the force and the nature of the case; but every suspect will be booked in, searched and booked out. Typically, he will be taken to the charge room where his particulars will be taken and where he will be searched. All property on his person will be listed and retained by the police until he is released. He will be invited to sign the list as a true record and will be asked whether he wants anyone informed of his whereabouts. (The police will need to contact the parent of juveniles and will ask whether anyone is at home.) Usually the police will wish to interview the suspect. They may do this straight away, but frequently there will be some delay before they are ready to proceed. During this period, juveniles may be detained in a detention room and adults in a cell. If the police charge the suspect, they will need to prepare a statement of his antecedents for the court, and may take fingerprints and photographs for their records before he is bailed or returned to the cells. The whole process can take as little as 30 minutes, but, in serious and exceptional cases, it may take longer than 24 hours.

Before deciding whether to charge a suspect, or inform him that he may be prosecuted, the police may need to interview witnesses and get statements from them; they may need to arrange an identity parade, or to check the premises from which they believe property was stolen; they may need to ask the suspect to accompany them while, with his consent, they search his house or car. In one case, which was observed in a pilot study, the police needed two days to check the alibi of a suspect who was eventually charged with robbing a bank. Enquiries are sometimes delayed because a suspect refuses to give his name and address, or is too drunk to assist the police. In cases involving juveniles, problems sometimes arise in contacting parents or persuading an angry father to attend the police station.

When a person is taken into custody, the police have a general obligation to bring him before a magistrates' court as soon as practicable. Under section 38 of the Magistrates' Courts Act 1952, as amended by the Bail Act 1976, a person taken into custody for an offence without a warrant shall be brought before a magistrates' court or bailed within 24 hours, unless the offence appears to the officer in charge of the station to be a serious one.

The time actually spent by suspects at the police station is shown in Table 2:2.

Table 2:2 Interval between arrival at the police station and being released or put into a cell after charging

Time at the police station (hours)	Suspects (Cumulative frequency)	
	No.	%
Up to 1	26	11.9
,, 2	60	27.5
,, 3	103	47.2
,, 6	157	72.0
,, 9	175	80.3
,, 12	191	87.6
,, 18	205	94.0
,, 24	215	98.6
,, 36	217	99.5
,, 48	218	100.0

Almost one half of suspects were dealt with in not more than 3 hours and approximately three quarters were disposed of within 6 hours. Only three were detained for more than 24 hours. The suspect who was detained longest was arrested on suspicion of having taken a motor vehicle without the consent of the owner. He had refused to give his name and address. At the station he refused to answer any questions. Enquiries eventually revealed his identity and that, although he had apparently acquired the car legitimately from a scrap-metal dealer, he was wanted in connection with a warrant of commitment to prison issued for non-payment of fines. He was released when his brother promptly paid the fines.

The time that a suspect spends in police custody is related to the nature of the offence under investigation. Over three quarters of persons suspected of theft from a store were dealt with in three hours or less, whereas just over half of the persons suspected of burglary were detained for more than 12 hours. The details are shown in Table 2:3.

Table 2:3 Interval between arrival at the police station and being released or put into a cell after charging by offence

Time at the police station (hours)	Burglary	Theft from store	Other theft	Wounding or assault	Other	Total
	Suspects %	Suspects %	Suspects %	Suspects %	Suspects %	Suspects %
Up to 3	17.4	77.3	53.1	43.2	22.6	47.2
— 12	30.4	22.7	37.5	52.3	58.5	40.4
Over 12	52.2	0.0	9.4	4.5	18.9	12.4
Total	100.0 (N = 23)	100.0 (N = 66)	100.0 (N = 32)	100.0 (N = 44)	100.0 (N = 53)	100.0 (N = 218)

Somewhat surprisingly, an analysis within each type of offence disclosed no obvious relationship between the time spent at the police station and the strength of the evidence against the suspect.

Despite having to wait for a relative or social worker to arrive, juveniles were generally dealt with more speedily than adults, as Table 2:4 shows. This is probably because they tended to be involved in less serious offences, most notably theft from stores.

Table 2:4 Interval between arrival at the police station and being released or put into a cell after charging by age

Time at the police station (hours)	Juvenile suspects %	Adult suspects %
Up to 3	78.0	38.1
— 12	20.0	46.4
Over 12	2.0	15.5
Total	100.0 (N = 50)	100.0 (N = 168)

The majority of suspects were detained in a cell or detention room when they were not actually being questioned or otherwise assisting the police with their enquiries at the station. One hundred and thirty four adults (80 per cent) were detained in a cell, and a further 12 (7 per cent) were detained in a detention room. Thirty four juveniles, (68 per cent) were detained in a detention room; none was detained in a cell. The time spent by adults and juveniles in a cell or detention room, prior to being released or detained after charging, is shown in Table 2:5

Table 2:5 Time spent in a cell or detention room by age

Time in cell or detention room (hours)	Juvenile suspects %	Adult suspects %
None	32.0	13.1
Up to 3	54.0	33.3
— 12	12.0	39.3
Over 12	2.0	14.3
Total	*100.0*	*100.0*
	(N = 50)	(N = 168)

CHAPTER 3

Contact with persons other than police officers

A person in custody at a police station may well feel isolated and dependent on the goodwill of the police, but detention at a police station does not completely sever a suspect's contact with his friends or legal adviser. The Administrative Directions accompanying the Judges' Rules stipulate that notices describing the rights and facilities available to persons in custody should be displayed at convenient and conspicuous places at police stations; that the attention of persons in custody should be drawn to these; that such persons should be informed orally of their rights, and that they should be allowed to speak on the telephone to a solicitor or friend, provided that no hindrance is likely to be caused to the process of investigation or the administration of justice. Supplementing the provisions of the Judges' Rules and Administrative Directions, s. 62 of the Criminal Law Act 1977 entitles a person who has been arrested and is being held in custody in a police station to have someone informed of his whereabouts with no more delay than is necessary in the interest of the investigation or prevention of crime or the apprehension of offenders.

All four of the police stations visited by the research team exhibited at least one notice informing persons in custody of their rights. Station A displayed a notice advising prisoners of their rights to inform someone of their arrest; to contact a solicitor and see him in private; to be examined by a doctor of their own choosing; to be admitted to bail; to refuse fingerprinting; and to apply for legal aid. This notice was displayed in 7 separate locations, including the charge room, interview rooms and corridors of the cell area. Station A also had a list of solicitors who were on call 24 hours a day, which was displayed in the charge room and several of the interview rooms. In contrast, Station D displayed only one notice. It was above the point where incoming suspects stood or sat when particulars were being taken. The notice was a large one and, although a suspect would normally have his back to it, the headings could be read by any officer addressing the prisoner from the charge room desk. There was no list of solicitors on display at Station D. Stations B and C, both displaying notices in several locations, fell between these two extremes. A list of solicitors was kept on the top of a filing cabinet in the charge room at Station C.

At Stations A and D, notices were given to suspects shortly after their arrival. The notice at Station A was comprehensive and included the right to contact a solicitor, but at Station D it dealt only with s. 62 of the Criminal Law

Act 1977. In some of the cases at these stations, notices were not handed to suspects: this happened in 30 per cent of the cases at station A and 50 per cent of the cases at Station D. At both stations juveniles were rarely handed a notice, and the difference reflects the higher proportion of juveniles at Station D.

Police officers did not make a practice of informing suspects orally of all their rights when they arrived at the police station. They preferred to deal with matters as they arose, so that, for example, a suspect would normally be cautioned when the police wished to interview him. An exception occurred at Station A. The suspect, a foreign visitor, was arrested for theft from an unattended vehicle and had been caught in the act. On arriving at the police station, he was handed a notice informing him of his rights. He told the officer who was dealing with the case that he could not read it, whereupon the officer read and explained the notice to him. The suspect did not want anyone told of his whereabouts, but expressed a wish to make a phone call to Malta, to see a doctor and a solicitor. He wanted to be admitted immediately to bail and said that he would refuse permission for his fingerprints to be taken. The suspect was unwilling to pay for the phone call and was persuaded that, as he was neither injured nor unwell, he did not need to see a doctor. He was allowed to see a solicitor, but was detained after being charged as he was of no fixed abode.

Contact with friends or relatives

When a child or young person under 17 is arrested, the police need to contact the parents, and should, as far as practicable, interview the young suspect only in the presence of a parent or guardian, or, in their absence, some person who is not a police officer and is of the same sex as the child. Adults are free to waive their right to have someone informed of their whereabouts and when they are interviewed they may only have a civilian present at the discretion of the police.

Police officers were conscientious in asking adult prisoners whether they wanted someone informed. Although no check was made on whether, and, if so, how promptly, the police were able to comply with such requests,[1] a record was kept of exchanges on the matter. The results are shown in Table 3:1.

Perhaps the most interesting result is that one half of the adults did not want anyone informed of their whereabouts. In most cases suspects gave no reason for declining, and the police asked for none. Some said that they preferred to break the news personally after their release, whilst others apparently hoped to keep the incident from their families and friends. Nine of the adult suspects were visited at the police station by a relative or friend.

In only two cases did the police not inform someone of the suspect's whereabouts and refuse permission for him to telephone a relative or friend. In

---

[1] Some information on this is available as a result of a separate procedure whereby the police send to the Home Office each month a return of the number of cases in which a request has not been complied with for four hours or more.

Table 3:1 Adult suspects only: whether the police offered or agreed to inform someone of the suspect's whereabouts.

Whether the police offered or agreed to inform someone of the suspect's whereabouts	Adult suspects	
	No.	%
Police offered - suspect agreed	35	20.9
Police offered - suspect refused	84	50.0
Suspect asked - police agreed	11	6.5
Neither the police nor the suspect was heard to raise the matter	38	22.6
Total	*168*	*100.0*

one of them, a man suspected of receiving stolen goods was brought to the police station at 5.50am. At 6am he was asked whether he wanted anyone informed of his whereabouts and he declined. At 12 noon, 3.40pm and 8.10pm he asked if he could contact his common-law wife. Each time he was told that he would be able to do so later. However, his wife knew of his whereabouts and had telephoned the police station herself. The police regarded the suspect as a professional criminal and were pursuing further enquiries.

In the other case, a man suspected of criminal damage was brought to the police station at 11.05pm. Within three minutes of his arrival, he had expressed a wish to contact his mother and a solicitor. Both requests were refused. He was drunk and had refused to give his name. The suspect was not interviewed. He was charged at 3.25am and returned to his cell.

In more than a third of the cases involving the 50 juvenile suspects, a parent or guardian was not available or refused to come to the police station, and in 6 of these cases no suitable adult came to the station. The details are shown in Table 3:2.

Table 3:2 Juvenile suspects only: non-police adults who attended the police station.

Non-police adults who attended the police station	Juvenile suspects	
	No.	%
Parent or guardian	31	62.0
Other relative	4	8.0
Social worker	6	12.0
Father of co-suspect	3	6.0
None	6	12.0
Total	*50*	*100.0*

It can be seen that in 35 cases (70 per cent) a relative attended; in 6 cases the local social services department supplied a social worker, and in 3 other cases the police made do with the father of a co-suspect. Of the 6 remaining suspects 4 were taken home (where they may have been interviewed), and one, who was almost 17, was dealt with alone at the station in deference to his request that his widowed mother should not be told. The parents of the sixth suspect refused to attend.

Table 3:3 shows that there was often a considerable delay between the arrival of a juvenile suspect at the police station and the arrival of a parent or other suitable person.

Table 3:3 Juvenile suspects only: interval between arrival of suspect and arrival of a non-police adult.

Interval (hours)	Juvenile suspects	
	No.	%
Up to one	13	29.5
- two	20	45.5
- three	3	6.8
Over three	8	18.2
Total[1]	*44*	*100.0*

[1] The total excludes 6 cases where no adult arrived.

Among the cases in which there was a long delay was that of a juvenile arrested during the night. His parents were contacted at 2am but refused to come to the police station. The social services department was contacted shortly afterwards and a social worker eventually arrived at 8.10am.

In none of the cases in which a parent or other suitable adult arrived within an hour was a juvenile interviewed in the absence of a civilian. Nine juveniles were interviewed in the absence of a suitable adult. In 3 cases the police were unable to contact any suitable adult who was able (or prepared) to come to the station within a reasonable time; in 2 cases suspects were anxious to talk to the police without their parents present (the police went along with this) and in 4 cases it was not apparent why the police proceeded with the interview before an adult arrived. Observers formed the impression that, in most cases, officers questioning juvenile suspects found it helpful to have a parent present. A responsible parent could encourage a child to tell the truth, though there was a risk that a confession made under even mild parental pressure could be held to be inadmissible. However, irate parents could cause problems: in one case a police officer intervened to stop a mother assaulting her 12 year old daughter with a slipper for having 'brought shame on the family'. It was evident that some young suspects were afraid of their parents and of being punished when they got home.

Contact with solicitors

The preamble to the Judges' Rules lays down the principle that 'every person at any stage of an investigation should be able to communicate and consult privately with a solicitor. This is so even if he is in custody provided that in such a case no unreasonable delay or hindrance is caused to the process of investigation or the administration of justice by his doing so'.[1]

Only one of the 50 juvenile suspects was visited at the police station by a solicitor. The suspect, a boy of 15, had been arrested with a friend for attempted theft of a car. Each denied the offence and blamed the other. Between three and four hours after the boy's arrival at the police station, his mother arrived with a solicitor. They were allowed a private meeting with the boy, after which he was interviewed in the presence of his mother and solicitor. During the interview, the solicitor took notes but did not advise. The boy denied the offence and was released into the custody of his mother to await the decision of the juvenile bureau.

Table 3:4 shows that in 84 per cent of the cases involving adult suspects the subject of access to a solicitor was not raised. In 5 per cent of cases the subject was raised by the police and in 11 per cent of cases it was raised by the suspect. The table also shows that in the majority of cases where suspects were offered facilities to contact a solicitor they declined, and that in the majority of cases where they requested such facilities they were granted.

Table 3:4 Adult suspects only: whether the police offered access to a solicitor or agreed to a solicitor being contacted.

Whether the police offered access to a solicitor or agreed to a solicitor being contacted	Adult suspects	
	No.	%
Police offered − suspect agreed	2	1.2
Police offered − suspect refused	6	3.6
Suspect asked − police agreed	13	7.7
Suspect asked − police refused	6	3.6
Neither police nor suspect raised the matter	141	83.9
Total	*168*	*100.0*

There is some evidence that the demand for solicitors may be increased by giving suspects leaflets informing them of their right to see a solicitor. At station A, where suspects were handed a notice advising them of this right, 21 per cent of adult suspects (11 out of 52) asked to see a solicitor, whereas only 7 per cent of adult suspects (8 out of 116) dealt with at the other police stations made such a request. Although the difference is statistically significant ($p < .05$), it would be unsound to draw general conclusions from only one police station, as local factors other than the notice might be involved.

In view of the claim, frequently made by policemen, that experienced criminals take advantage of the Rules in order to avoid conviction, it was thought that the more experienced suspects might be more ready to stand on their rights and demand a solicitor. It was known from enquiries made by police that 90 of the adult suspects had a criminal record and that 55 had no

[1] Principle (c), *Judges' Rules and Administrative Directions to the Police*. Home Office Circular No. 89/1978. HMSO, London.

record. (In 23 cases it was not known, when observers enquired, whether the suspect had previously been in trouble.) Twenty per cent (18) of the adult suspects with a criminal record asked to see a solicitor and only 2 per cent (1) of those with no record made such a request. The difference is statistically significant (p < .01). It is also apparent that those facing serious charges were more likely than others to ask for a solicitor. Among 22 adults arrested for burglary, 8 asked to see a solicitor. However, requests for legal advice were not confined to serious cases: they covered the full range of offences, including shoplifting, handling, taking a motor vehicle without consent, deception, minor assault, criminal damage and possession of drugs.

When a person in police custody asks to see a solicitor, it does not necessarily follow that he will be allowed to contact one. Table 3:4 shows that in six of the 19 cases where an adult suspect asked to see a solicitor, the police refused permission. Three of these suspects had refused to give their names — two of the three were under the influence of drink — and a further three were told that they could see one later — in the morning, after particulars had been taken, or after being interviewed. One of these had been arrested near the scene of a burglary. There were witnesses who could testify that he was with a group of young adults who had broken a shop window and stolen articles of clothing from the display; but the extent of his involvement was not clear. During the first interview, in which he asked to see a solicitor, he admitted being with the others, but denied taking any part in the offence. In a second interview, during which no solicitor was present, he made a written statement admitting that he had kicked the shop window. He was later charged with burglary.

Although the police gave permission for 15 adult suspects to contact a solicitor, only 9 (5 per cent of the total number) were seen at the police station by a solicitor. One suspect changed his mind and decided that he would contact a solicitor after he was released. Another found that the solicitor was out when he telephoned at 4.50pm. The solicitor rang back at 9pm, by which time the suspect was being released.

Of the 9 solicitors who attended the police station, 2 arrived before the suspect had been interviewed and 7 arrived after the suspect had been interviewed.

Among the cases in which a solicitor did not arrive until after the suspect had been interviewed was one connected with the investigation of a major burglary. The police had approached the public for assistance and the information which they had received had led to the arrest of a young man. The suspect had been acquitted in the Crown Court on several occasions and was regarded by the police as a sophisticated criminal. He was interviewed twice in connection with the current investigation. He asked to see a solicitor at the beginning of the first interview and a solicitor arrived within an hour. During the first interview, he admitted a minor offence (possession of a lamp) and signed a written confession to this offence; but he denied involvement in the burglary. After he had had a private meeting with his solicitor, he was interviewed a second time by one of the two detectives working on the case. On being cautioned at the beginning of this interview, he replied: 'I wish to exercise my right of silence'. Questioned obliquely, he gave information which the investigating officer regarded as incriminating. He was bailed to come back to the station after the police had made further enquiries. At the police station he had twice admitted off the record — once to a detective and once to a member of the research team — that he had committed the burglary, but his confession was never made in the presence of more than one person.

Another case in which a solicitor did not arrive until the suspect had been interviewed concerned a young woman in her twenties who was suspected of burglary. She was interviewed twice. She had asked to see a solicitor during the first interview, but she was not seen until the police had finished questioning her. She had come voluntarily to the police station to collect her clothes and was arrested on arrival. On a previous occasion her boyfriend had been found wandering in the streets at night with a television set, which the police believed was stolen from a shop with a broken window. He denied having been near the shop. His alibi was that he had been with his girlfriend. His girlfriend was questioned and the police took clothing for forensic examination. Examination of glass fragments found on the clothing suggested that the fragments were from the shop window and proved that her account of how they came to be on her clothing was untrue. The prosecution case would have been strengthened by a confession to corroborate the forensic evidence. The interviews with the woman at the police station were relaxed and friendly. The police constable questioning her stressed that the overwhelming evidence of guilt would ensure her conviction and that, by pleading guilty, mitigating factors could be brought out which would result in a lighter sentence. In both interviews she repeatedly denied the offence. She was not persuaded to be more forthcoming about what happened and was charged after she had seen a solicitor. On asking the investigating officer why he had not agreed to let her see a solicitor earlier, the observer was told that there was no need to have a solicitor; that a solicitor was not there when the crime was committed and would only impede the investigation by telling her to say nothing. Evidently the officer, like a number of others, felt that, although there was no guarantee that a suspect would answer police questions or make damaging remarks in the absence of a solicitor, the presence of a solicitor made it more likely that the interview would prove fruitless.

The two cases in which a solicitor arrived before the suspect was interviewed help to explain the officer's view. One suspect was caught stealing from an unattended car. He was advised that he should admit the offence which the police could prove; that he should make no admission in respect of other property which the police had found in his car, and that he should not make a written statement. The other suspect was believed to have committed a burglary. The police postponed their interview with him so that he could first see his solicitor. When he was eventually questioned, he replied: 'My solicitor advised me not to say anything.'

CHAPTER 4

The caution and the right to silence

The Judges' Rules make it clear that a police officer may question anyone whom he thinks may be able to give useful information, but that as soon as he has evidence which gives reasonable grounds for suspecting that a person has committed an offence, he must caution him. Rule II requires that the caution be given in the following terms: 'You are not obliged to say anything unless you wish to do so but what you say may be put into writing and given in evidence.' Rule III (a) requires that when a person is charged or informed that he may be prosecuted for an offence a similar warning is given to him.

The cautioning of suspects by the police about their right to silence is favoured by those who believe that persons in custody should be protected against self-incrimination, and criticised by others who regard the right to silence as a hindrance to successful investigation. For this reason it is one of the most controversial features of police interrogation. The aims of this chapter are to show to what extent the police safeguard the rights of suspects by cautioning and how often suspects take advantage of their right to refuse to answer questions.

It appeared to observers that the normal practice followed by the police was to caution a suspect at the time of arrest, at the beginning of any interview at the police station, and again if and when he was charged.

Two hundred and four suspects had been arrested prior to their arrival at the police station, and 14 suspects had not been arrested. In each case, where a suspect had been arrested and brought to the police station, a member of the research team enquired whether the suspect had been cautioned before he arrived at the station. In only 21 (10 per cent) of the 204 cases, where the suspect had been arrested and taken to the police station, was the observer told that the suspect had not been cautioned prior to arrival. Although observers could not verify the accuracy of this figure, they had no reason to doubt it. Cautioning at the arrest stage clearly seems to be a common practice, and the fact that 10 per cent had not been cautioned at this stage does not signify any breach of standard procedure. Cautioning a suspect at the time of arrest may not be practicable where, for example, the suspect is violent or drunk. Furthermore, it is not always strictly necessary: although a caution should be given when a police officer has evidence which would afford reasonable grounds for suspecting that a person has committed an offence, this stage is not necessarily contemporaneous with the arrest stage, because the suspicion on which an arrest is made, albeit reasonable, need not arise from evidence that is admissible in a court of law.[1] Whether a suspect is cautioned at the police station depends on whether he has been arrested prior to arrival, whether the police wish to interview him and whether he is charged.

All 14 suspects who had not been arrested prior to arrival at the police station were cautioned there. Thirteen were cautioned prior to being interviewed and one, who was not interviewed, was cautioned on being arrested at the station.

Thirty of the 204 suspects who had been arrested and brought to the police station were not interviewed there. A typical case in this group involved a girl of 15 suspected of shoplifting. She had been seen by a store detective to take some brassières and leave the store without paying for them. She was detained and a police officer was called. At the store, the officer asked her if she had intended to steal the goods. She replied that she had. She was arrested, cautioned and brought to the police station. No formal interview or further caution was thought necessary before she was charged. In this group of 30 suspects, only three were cautioned at the police station on an occasion apart from any formal charging. In each of these three cases, it appeared that the police wished to interview the suspect, but were thwarted because the suspect refused to answer any questions about the offence. In two cases the police had sufficient evidence to charge the suspect, but in the third case there was insufficient evidence and the suspect was released.

Of the remaining 174 suspects who were arrested, taken to the police station and interviewed there, 4 – all of whom had been cautioned at the time of arrest – were not cautioned at the station until the beginning of a second interview, and 27 were not cautioned at the station on any occasion apart from the formalities of any charging. Three of the 27 had not been cautioned prior to arrival at the police station. The details of these cases are shown below.

The suspect, a girl aged 18, was arrested on suspicion of theft of cash from a handbag. She was a student and part-time cleaner, and had been found at the scene of the offence. Apparently, she had no right to be there, so the police were called. She was arrested, taken to the police station and questioned by a woman police constable. In the words of the investigating officer, who explained to the observer that without a confession there would be insufficient evidence to substantiate a charge: 'It was a cough to nothing'. The girl denied the offence and the case was reported to a senior officer for a decision whether to prosecute.

The suspect, a man aged 26, was arrested after the police had been called to a pub fight. At the police station he was questioned with a view to finding out what had happened and who was involved. He gave the names of those who had started the fight and was bailed to return to the police station after the police had completed their enquiries.

The suspect, a man aged 23, was believed to be involved in the same pub fight. He was arrested and taken to the police station, where he denied all knowledge of the fracas and refused to answer any questions. He too was bailed to return to the police station.

---

[1] *R. v. Virtue* [1973] Q.B. 678.

All suspects who were charged were formally cautioned as part of the charging procedure. This final caution invariably terminated questioning, though accused persons were occasionally asked about other offences. Only one was questioned about the offence with which he had been charged. The suspect had been charged with the theft of a car safety harness and was asked: 'What did you want it for if you haven't got a car?'

Of the 187 suspects who were interviewed at the police station, 147 (79 per cent) were cautioned at the beginning of the first interview, 8 (4 per cent) were cautioned during the first interview (but not within the first five minutes), and 4 (2 per cent) were first cautioned at the station at the beginning of a second interview. (As mentioned above, in 27 cases the suspect was not cautioned when he was questioned at the station. In one further case the observer was not present during the interview and was unable to ascertain whether the suspect had been cautioned.) What follows is an account of the cautioning of 159 interviewed suspects in the first interview in which they were cautioned at the police station.

The wording of the caution is analysed in Table 4:1.

Table 4:1 Suspects cautioned at the beginning of or during an interview: wording of the caution

Wording of the caution	Suspects	
	No.	%
Standard form	106	66.6
Standard form, partly paraphrased	10	6.3
Officer's own words	37	23.3
Cautioned as per written statement	2	1.3
Not known	4	2.5
Total	*159*	*100.0*

In two thirds of cases the caution was delivered by the book: 'You are not obliged to say anything unless you wish to do so, but what you say may be put into writing and given in evidence.' An officer might preface the standard form by saying: 'I have to tell you that . . .' or 'I remind you that . . .'. In a further 6 per cent of cases the standard form was slightly modified to make it sound more natural. For example, officers occasionally began: 'You don't have to say anything, but . . .'. In almost a quarter of cases officers preferred their own form of words. Cne suspect was warned: 'I know you're involved in this, so I'm telling you, you don't have to say anything and, if you do, it'll be used in court.' Sometimes all that was offered was a reminder that the suspect was still under caution, or a cursory: 'You know you don't have to say anything, OK?' Table 4:1 shows that, during the interview, two suspects were first cautioned in connection with the formalities of taking a written statement.

In only one case did the observer consider that the caution was not delivered clearly, though in several cases the way in which the caution was delivered, or

73

the manner of its phrasing, seemed to present the right to silence as an option which the suspect was not seriously expected to entertain.

Some police officers were rather baffled by the logic of cautioning persons whom they were expected to question. Other officers, however, found the caution helpful as a reminder to suspects of the gravity of the situation. In 23 cases (14 per cent) suspects were actually asked whether they understood the caution.

Often the suspect showed no perceptible response to the caution, but in most cases the caution was acknowledged with a perfunctory nod, or a polite 'Yes' or 'Mm'. Only 9 suspects (5 per cent of those cautioned at the beginning of or during an interview) said or indicated by their response that they did not understand. Seven of these suspects queried the standard form of caution. In two cases the query followed an enquiry by the investigating officer.

Fourteen suspects (9 per cent) refused to answer some or all questions after caution during the first interview in which they were cautioned. Six refused to answer all questions of substance and 8 refused to answer some questions. Two suspects had refused to answer questions before they were cautioned and were therefore either aware of their rights or simply not disposed to cooperate. On only two occasions was it clear that it was the caution itself which encouraged silence – once when the suspect was cautioned slowly and deliberately, and once when a young police constable asked a juvenile suspect why he had made no attempt to answer any questions. The juvenile replied: 'You said that I didn't have to say anything.' Undeterred, the officer explained: 'But that would look suspicious wouldn't it?'

Most of the questions that suspects refused to answer related to their part in the offence under investigation, but in one case they related to the part played by other persons. In only 4 out of 22 cases where the suspect refused to answer questions did the police immediately drop the matter.

Where suspects had been cautioned and had waived their right to silence, the answers given in the course of an interview were not necessarily helpful or truthful. In over a third of cases (where suspects had not refused to answer any questions) replies were sometimes vague or evasive, and in at least another 12 per cent of cases they were untruthful.[1]

An analysis of all interviews with the 187 suspects who were interviewed at the police station revealed that 4 per cent (7) of those interviewed refused to answer *all* questions of substance and 8 per cent (15) refused to answer some questions. Thus a total of 12 per cent of suspects questioned at the police station exercised their right to silence to some degree. Of the seven suspects who refused to answer all questions, four were eventually prosecuted and convicted and three were released. The four who were prosecuted had been caught in the act whereas the three who were released had been arrested on somewhat weaker evidence.

Only 5 per cent of 38 suspects under 17 and 7 per cent of 59 aged 17 to 20 exercised their right to silence to some degree whereas 18 per cent of the 90

---

[1] Observers would not claim that they could always tell when a suspect was being untruthful. They merely inferred that, when a suspect gave two contradictory accounts, at least one version was false.

remaining suspects, aged 21 or over, did so. (A comparison of all suspects under 21 with those aged 21 or over shows a statistically significant difference ($p < .05$). Of 70 suspects who were interviewed and were known not to have a criminal record, only 6 per cent exercised their right to some degree;[1] but among 97 suspects interviewed at the police station who were known to have a criminal record 17 per cent did. The difference is again statistically significant ($p < .05$). Five of the 23 persons suspected of burglary refused to answer some questions when they were interviewed at the police station. These results clearly show that the large majority of suspects in all age groups do not exercise their right to silence, but that older and more experienced suspects are more likely than others to do so.

There is of course, no guarantee that answers given by a suspect, whether under caution or not, will be truthful; but it is arguable that an investigating officer would have a better chance of uncovering the truth, without applying undue pressure, if he was not put in a position where he was obliged first to tell the suspect that it was not necessary to answer his questions and then to devise ways of persuading the suspect to answer.

---

[1] Four suspects who were known not to have a criminal record refused to answer certain questions. None refused to answer all questions.

CHAPTER 5

Interviews with suspects at the police station

One hundred and eighty seven suspects (86 per cent) were interviewed at the police station: 140 were interviewed once, 41 were interviewed twice, 2 were interviewed three times, 3 had four interviews and one was interviewed on five occasions. An interview was defined as a number of probing questions, the answers to which could be incriminating if the suspect had committed the offence under investigation, and included the taking of a written statement under caution. Although this definition did not preclude observers from recording as an interview any prolonged and pertinent exchange, regardless of the stage of proceedings at the police station, it was found that, in practice, the interview was almost always conducted as a separate exercise, usually in a room set aside for the purpose. It therefore seems that questioning which observers recorded as constituting an interview would correspond closely to what the police would regard as a formal interview.

The importance placed on the formal interview appears to vary between police stations. At three of the police stations visited, over 90 per cent of suspects were interviewed at the station but, at the fourth, only 37 per cent of suspects were interviewed. At the fourth station the majority of those who were not interviewed had admitted the offence when they were arrested, and a relatively high proportion of the cases involved shoplifting. However, it is not considered that these factors entirely explain the low interview rate, which appears to reflect a difference in the practice of the station.

The point of interviewing suspects sometimes seemed to be purely procedural, since the police already knew what had happened. For example, one suspect was interviewed after he had been brought in for obstructing the police. In connection with a separate incident, the police interviewed a suspect who had insulted a police officer and, in another case, they interviewed a suspect who had sworn at a police officer and had held on to a friend whom the officer was trying to arrest. However, even where the police knew what had happened, interviewing a suspect was not necessarily a mere formality. It was sometimes apparent that the police wanted a written statement. In cases of dishonesty, such as theft from a store or handling, investigating officers took pains to establish whether the suspect had a guilty intent or guilty knowledge. Although, in such cases, a denial would not necessarily result in the charge being refused (if the police were satisfied that an offence had been committed), an admission would clearly meet the standard of proof which would be required if the suspect were to be successfully prosecuted. Sometimes the main purpose of an interview was to ask suspects about other offences, about co-suspects, or about accomplices still at large.

The police were more likely to interview persons suspected of serious offences than those suspected of minor crimes. Every person suspected of burglary was interviewed at the police station, but slightly less than four fifths of those suspected of theft from a store were interviewed. For some of the less serious offences, the data suggest that the probability of being interviewed at the police station depended on the strength of the evidence. For example, all 9 suspects seen in the company of shoplifters were interviewed. Similarly, among cases of wounding or assault, only 16 of the 22 suspects identified by reliable witnesses were interviewed, whereas all but one of the 21 suspects found at or near the scene of a disturbance were interviewed.

Observers asked the police what they hoped to gain by interviewing the suspect. In most cases (86 per cent) they said it was simply to find out what had happened or to get the suspect's side of the story; in 7 per cent of cases they said it was to establish whether there was guilty intent or guilty knowledge and, in a further 5 per cent of cases, both these reasons were mentioned. To establish guilty intent was spontaneously mentioned as a reason for interview in nearly a quarter of shoplifting cases. It was less frequently mentioned in other cases of dishonesty.

Typically, the interview was a means of testing or supplementing existing evidence. It often, as will be shown in the next Chapter, served to strengthen the case for the prosecution. In 14 cases (8 per cent) the police said that the interview helped to show that the suspect was not involved in the offence, and in a number of other cases it showed that there was considerable doubt as to the suspect's guilt and that the case should be dropped. The interview could also be helpful in yielding information about other offences or other suspects.

The aims of what follows in this chapter are to describe initial interviews at the station, with reference to the tactics employed and the results obtained; to examine the taking of written statements under caution, and to consider the reasons for and the nature of subsequent interviews at the police station.

Initial interviews with suspects

In the vast majority of cases, the initial interview was conducted free from other distractions. Seventy one per cent of first interviews were conducted in an interview room; 11 per cent were conducted in some other room, such as the CID office; 10 per cent were conducted in a cell or detention room, and 3 per cent in the charge room. In three of the stations visited, at least one room was set aside for questioning suspects.

Interviews were, for the most part, short. Table 5:1 shows that four-fifths of them were concluded within half an hour, and that only 5 per cent lasted more than 45 minutes.

The maximum number of officers present in any interview was four. Normally only one or two officers were present during questioning. In 37 per cent of initial interviews only one officer was present, and in 58 per cent two officers were present. Often, where two officers were present, the second

Table 5:1 Duration of initial interviews

Duration of interview	Suspects	
	No.	%
Not more than 5 minutes	25	13.4
More than 5 minutes to 10 minutes	42	22.5
− 15 minutes	30	16.0
− 30 minutes	52	27.8
− 45 minutes	28	15.0
− 1 hour	7	3.7
− 2 hours	3	1.6
Total	*187*	*100.0*

officer took no part in questioning: his main role appeared to be to provide corroboration or, occasionally, to take notes. In most of the interviews with juveniles a person other than a police officer was also present.

The police face obvious difficulties in trying to persuade people to reveal incriminating information about themselves or their friends, though these are often not as great as might be expected. Suspects are under great psychological pressure when they have committed an offence and are confronted by the police for questioning. Confession provides a way to relieve the tension. Often, the evidence against the suspect is overwhelming (at least in his own eyes) and he may feel that denial would only prolong the ordeal to no purpose. If an offence is not readily admitted, the police can employ a range of tactics to increase the pressure on the suspect to confess or to remove the shame or guilt which may inhibit a confession. The skill of the questioner can therefore be an important ingredient in securing the information needed to construct a case, particularly where other evidence is inconclusive.

Observers were asked to note any tactics that were used to encourage a suspect to part with information. In 111 cases (60 per cent of initial interviews) at least one tactic was identified.

The most common tactic, cited in 22 per cent of initial interviews, was that of pointing out contradictions in the suspect's account, or contradictions between the suspect's account and that of co-suspects or other witnesses. In such cases, the police could sometimes give a sharper edge to their questioning by stressing the greater reliability of those who did not have the suspect's incentive to prevaricate.

In 13 per cent of initial interviews the police stressed the overwhelming evidence against the suspect. The evidence was usually presented in a way that showed the suspect in the most incriminating light, which made denial seem pointless.

The police often worked hard to establish rapport with the suspect and to create a relaxed atmosphere, conducive to easy conversation. (The suspect was usually addressed by his first name.) It was clear that, in at least 11 per cent of initial interviews, the police made a point of engaging the suspect in general, friendly chat, of cracking jokes, offering a cigarette or a cup of tea. The police were not above resorting to flattery, as in a case involving an old hand arrested by a young uniformed officer. After a word of advice from his superiors, the officer adopted an approach suitably respectful of the suspect's true professional status, and apologised for rough treatment at the time of arrest: 'Sorry I was a bit rough with you earlier − I didn't realise who you were, but I've been put straight now.' The suspect responded by admitting the offence.

In 15 per cent of initial interviews the police appeared to bluff or hint that other evidence would be forthcoming. This usually involved their telling the suspect that the truth would inevitably emerge, so implying that honest answers would merely provide a short cut to a foregone conclusion. Occasionally the police might have exaggerated the strength of the evidence which they were likely to assemble. Where further evidence would genuinely be forthcoming, through, for example, forensic tests on clothing, the suspect would again be told that there was no point in withholding the truth.

In 6 per cent of initial interviews the police belittled either the offence itself or the suspect's part in it. This tactic was typically applied where the suspect was ashamed of his conduct or had exaggerated ideas about the severity with which a trivial offence would be viewed by the court.

If the police felt that a suspect was being obstructive and that the information he could provide would be particularly useful, more coercive tactics were sometimes used. In 7 per cent of initial interviews the police hinted at the possibility of detention for a long period. Typically, the police would say: 'You'll have to stay here until we've sorted all this out.' The message was clearly that it was within the suspect's power to speed up the process. Occasionally the pressure was stronger, as in a case involving a suspect who refused to answer any questions. The suspect was told that he would stay in the cell for some time if he was uncooperative. It was an empty threat: although he remained uncooperative, he was charged and released soon after the interview.

On three occasions the very act of returning a suspect to the cell triggered an admission. Preceded by a denial and followed by a confession, the trip to the cell was no more than a brief interruption in the interview. Whilst the outcome was doubtless gratifying to the police, it is difficult to judge whether the police had attempted to secure a confession by this means. However, there was another case where it was clear that the suspect had been returned to the cell in order to secure his cooperation. In this instance, the police wanted a written statement and the suspect was anxious to be released quickly. When he refused to make a statement in the first interview, the police said: 'Right, back to the cells.' He made a statement in a second interview 20 minutes later.

In 4 per cent of initial interviews the police either told the suspect that in helping them he would be helping himself − since the court would take account of any cooperation he gave − or stressed the damage that the suspect might do to his own case by pleading not guilty and wasting the court's time. In a further 2 per cent of initial interviews, the advantages of admitting other offences so that they could be taken into consideration − the tic procedure − were explained.[1] Sometimes other offences were quite readily admitted, but in

---

[1] The tic procedure enables the court, when imposing sentence, to take into consideration similar untried offences which the defendant admits. Such offences cannot subsequently be made the subject of separate charges.

these cases the police made a point of encouraging the suspect to put his mind at ease and make a fresh start. The suspect would be depicted in some idyllic scene, which is suddenly shattered by the arrival of a police officer who arrests him for some past crime. At little if any cost to himself, he could admit it now and wipe the slate clean. Although this tactic was rarely used in first interviews, it was not uncharacteristic of later ones.

Questioning was often a skilled and difficult task, but in 40 per cent of initial interviews no special tactics were noted. In most of these cases the suspect readily admitted the offence, or provided an explanation which absolved him. In other cases the police appeared to feel that they stood to gain very little from the interview or vigorous questioning. When the police applied psychological pressure – they never resorted to the use or threat of physical violence – it was generally done to counter a suspect's resistance to giving truthful answers or because they were uncertain of a suspect's guilt.

Information about offences other than those for which the suspect had been arrested was forthcoming in 14 per cent of initial interviews at the police station. (In second interviews the corresponding figure was 36 per cent.)[1]

In 39 per cent of initial interviews the suspects gave incriminating information about other persons, usually co-suspects. In 6 per cent of initial interviews suspects gave exculpatory information about other persons. Exculpatory information was quite frequently given in cases where several people had been arrested in connection with a disturbance and where the police were trying to sort out who was responsible.

Table 5:2 shows whether, during the course of the initial interview at the police station, the suspect made a confession, an admission, or a denial. In this and subsequent tables, an admission refers to an incriminating statement which fell short of a full confession: it includes for example, a statement by a suspect, who had initially denied assault, that he might have hit someone who could have been the complainant.

Table 5:2 Suspects interviewed at the police station: whether the suspect made a confession, an admission, or a denial during the initial interview.

Outcome of initial interview	Suspects	
	No.	%
Confession	78	41.7
Admission	33	17.6
Denial	65	34.8
Neither confession, admission, nor denial	11	5.9
Total	187	100.0

Fifty nine per cent of suspects confessed to the offence under investigation, or made a damaging admission, and 35 per cent of suspects denied the offence.

---

[1] Asking about other offences was fairly standard in cases of dishonesty.

80

The remaining 6 per cent said nothing or were too drunk to say anything coherent.

Written statements

A total of 52 suspects (28 per cent of those who were interviewed) made a written statement at some stage during their period of detention at the police station. One station accounted for two thirds of these statements. A statement was more likely to be made in a serious case than a trivial one: 13 of the 23 persons suspected for burglary made one. Written statements were generally made at the invitation of the police. Most officers who took a statement said that the object was to strengthen the prosecution case or to help the court. It was usually put to the suspect that the statement would give him a chance to put his side of the story.

Generally, a suspect was only asked whether he was prepared to make a statement after he had admitted an offence. It is therefore not surprising that in 95 per cent of cases the statement contained a confession or an admission. In only two cases was the offence denied in a written statement: in one of these, the statement implicated a co-suspect; in the other, it was helpful in determining whether to prosecute, as the police were genuinely in doubt as to the guilty intent of the suspect. In one other case, the statement, made at the suspect's own request, amounted to a tirade against the police.

The taking of a written statement under caution was not normally a lengthy procedure: only 5 per cent of statements took longer than 30 minutes, and 60 per cent were completed within 15 minutes. The police would ask the suspect whether he would like to write the statement himself or would prefer to have someone write it for him. In most cases (84 per cent), the suspect opted to dictate his statement. The statement was in all cases signed by the suspect, who usually wrote the final certificate.

Six of the 52 suspects who made a written statement received no assistance from the police, and 23 (almost one half) received neutral assistance on matters such as spelling, how to begin the statement and what was relevant. In 15 cases the police went a little further by recapitulating material points for inclusion and ensuring that admissions were explicit. In 7 of the remaining 8 cases[1] the police took a much more active part in wording the statement. For the most part, this involved their wording the statement on the basis of previous discussion. In one case, the officer composed a statement for a tearful and incoherent juvenile who appeared to be incapable of making his own statement. In another, the police officer started a second interview with a surly and aggressive youth by saying: 'You said you wanted to make a statement.' The officer proceeded to compose a highly incriminating statement based on remarks made, sometimes inadvertently, in the first interview. Sometimes the police suggested that the statement should end with some sort of apology – which left no room for doubt that an apology was due. Although the voluntariness of some of the written statements might clearly be

---

[1] The making of one statement was not witnessed by an observer.

questioned, in no case did the observer consider that a statement was materially false.

Second and subsequent interviews

Forty seven suspects (one quarter of those interviewed at the police station) were interviewed on two or more occasions. Sometimes the point of a subsequent interview was to obtain a written confession, but other factors also had a bearing on the decision to interview a suspect more than once.

Nearly half the persons interviewed at the police station were suspected of committing an offence jointly with at least one other person. This occasionally gave rise to the need to resolve conflicting accounts by re-interviewing co-suspects or gave the police an opportunity to confront a suspect with additional evidence. The seriousness of the offence also appeared to influence the decision to re-interview a suspect. Two thirds of persons suspected of burglary were interviewed more than once. The co-operativeness of the suspect was also relevant. Among 140 suspects who were interviewed only once, 6 per cent refused to answer at least some questions: among 47 suspects who were interviewed on two or more occasions 23 per cent refused to answer at least some questions during the first interview. Forty four per cent of suspects who were interviewed only once, compared with 34 per cent of those who were interviewed more than once, made a confession in the first interview.

Second and subsequent interviews were, in many respects, not very different from first ones. They were more often conducted in a cell or detention room. There was little difference in the number of police officers present, although, where two officers were present, it was rather more likely that both would be involved in questioning. When a suspect was cautioned in a second or subsequent interview the officer was more likely to use his own form of words. For the most part, the tactics employed were much the same as in first interviews, with one notable exception: the expediency of admitting other offences was stressed in 16 per cent of later interviews, compared with 2 per cent of first interviews. 'I know nobody gets caught first time – so does the judge', advised one experienced officer. Often, where the suspect had confessed in a previous interview to the offence for which he had been arrested, and this tactic was used, the main purpose of the interview was to persuade the suspect to admit other offences.

Six persons, five of whom were suspected of burglary, were interviewed more than twice. These cases are described briefly below.

The suspect was interviewed four times. He had been arrested for burglary at the hotel where he worked where he had been caught red handed stealing food. The purpose of the interviews was mainly to find out about other offences and the name of his accomplice. In the first interview the suspect was persuaded to disclose how much he expected to make from the crime. The police told him that he was being exploited by his accomplice, who would make far more than him, and played down his own role by saying that it was his accomplice whom they really wanted. Later interviews covered similar ground in more detail. The final interview took place after his accomplice had been brought in and fresh evidence had come to light. The police then tried unsuccessfully to persuade him to admit to further offences in the light of this new evidence.

The suspect was interviewed on three occasions. He had been found in enclosed premises and was eventually charged with burglary. Although the first interview was quite straightforward and the police secured a confession, he was interviewed again to find out about other offences. Several were admitted. The third interview involved only the taking of a written statement.

The suspect was interviewed three times. In the first interview he refused to answer any questions related to the offence (burglary). After the police had obtained an admission from a co-suspect, he was much more forthcoming and the thrust of questioning switched to other offences. After confessing to previous offences, he was invited to work as an informer. He responded by telling the officer about thefts committed by others. The third interview involved the taking of a written statement.

The suspect, who was interviewed five times, was found in a car which was registered as scrapped. The police believed it was stolen. He would not give his name, or any details about himself, and refused to answer all questions throughout the five interviews. Other enquiries, which involved considerable police effort, eventually bore fruit when he was identified by a woman who knew him. The reason for withholding his name then became apparent. He had been sentenced to 113 days imprisonment for non-payment of fines and a warrant for his arrest had been issued. Ironically, the car had been bought legitimately from a scrap dealer. The documents were waiting to be processed at the licensing centre.

The suspect had been arrested with others for burglary and interviewed four times. A shop window had been broken by kicking and clothes had been taken. The first interview was unfruitful. When confronted with the prospect of returning to his cell the suspect said: 'OK, I'll tell the truth.' He failed to live up to his promise. The second interview was no better, but the more he talked the more contradictory his story became. The third interview led to a confession: 'I did it, I threw half a brick through the window. My friend did nothing.' (His friend was due to be married the next day, so there was a strong incentive to absolve him.) The confession was rejected: 'Bollocks', said the incredulous officer, smiling. (A false confession was not enough: the officer wanted the truth.) Eventually his story matched those of co-suspects in all essentials. The fourth interview simply involved the taking of a written statement.

The suspect was one of five persons arrested in connection with the burglary described immediately above. He was also interviewed four times. He maintained throughout that he took no part in the burglary, and the interviews helped to clear him.

To summarise, interviews at the police station took place after the police had obtained some evidence of guilt. There was therefore pressure on all suspects either to admit the offence or to convince the police of their innocence and so save themselves further inconvenience. Additional pressure was sometimes applied by the police through a range of usually subtle, occasionally coercive, tactics. However, there was no indication that the police were interested in a confession at the expense of the truth: the lasting impression is that the police wanted the suspect to help them to establish what actually happened; who was involved; when the incident occurred; and why it occurred. In practice, interviews often did no more than confirm evidence which was already available to the police. This meant that they did not as a rule yield dramatic new insights into a case, but rather served to test whether the police were on the right course. Further consideration of the usefulness of interviews at the police station is given in the following chapter.

CHAPTER 6

The contribution of questioning to the detection of crime

In nearly 9 out of 10 cases, suspects were interviewed at the police station and, in most of the remaining cases, some kind of significant interchange short of a full interview took place between the suspect and the police either before their arrival at the station or subsequently. The purpose of this chapter is to take stock of what the police gained by questioning suspects and to assess the contribution of questioning to the detection of crime.

The nature of the study precluded observers from seeing what happened before a suspect arrived at the station. However, observers asked whether a suspect had been questioned before arrival and whether he or she had given information that was helpful to the police. Ninety three suspects had either been questioned or, less commonly, had given unsolicited information before they arrived at the station. Of these, 56 said something that the police felt would assist them in securing a conviction, bringing additional charges or by providing some sort of intelligence or information about other suspects. Of the 31 suspects who were not interviewed at the police station, 12 had admitted the offence before they arrived there.

Table 6:1 shows that, in the course of questioning, 48 per cent of the 187 suspects who were interviewed at the police station made a full confession and 13 per cent made a damaging admission falling short of a full confession. In just over 60 per cent of cases, therefore, the police elicited either a confession or some sort of incriminating statement.

Table 6:1 Suspects interviewed at the police station: Whether, during any interview, the suspect made a confession or an admission.

Outcome of interviews(s)	Suspects	
	No.	%
Confession	89	47.6
Admission	25	13.4
Neither confession nor admission	73	39.0
Total	*187*	*100.0*

Suspects with a criminal record were less likely than others to make a confession or an admission. Among 97 interviewed suspects who were known

85

to have a criminal record, 59 per cent made a confession or an admission; among 70 interviewed suspects with no criminal record, 76 per cent made a confession or an admission. The difference is statistically significant (p < .05). Full details are shown in Table 6:2.

Table 6:2 Suspects interviewed at the police station: Whether, during any interview, the suspect made a confession or an admission by criminal record.

Outcome of interview(s)	Criminal record	No criminal record
	Suspects %	Suspects %
Confession	47.4	57.1
Admission	11.3	18.6
Neither confession nor admission	41.2	24.3
Total[1]	*100.0*	*100.0*
	(N = 97)	*(N = 70)*

[1]Twenty cases were excluded where the criminal record of the suspect was not known

Suspects aged 21 or over were significantly less likely to admit responsibility than younger suspects: 53 per cent of 90 suspects aged 21 or over, compared with 68 per cent of 97 suspects under 21 made a confession or an admission (p < .05). Almost four-fifths (30) of the 38 juvenile suspects interviewed made a confession or admission. Suspects who were employed also appeared to be less likely than others to admit responsibility, but, after allowance had been made for age, the difference was not statistically significant.

The usefulness of a confession or an admission to the police depends on the strength of other evidence against the suspect. Where the other evidence is weak, a confession or an admission would enable the police to clear up a crime which would otherwise remain unsolved, but, where the other evidence is strong, the main value of a confession or an admission would simply be to strengthen the case for the prosecution. There were cases where a confession or an admission was the only direct evidence against the suspect. Three of 9 suspects who were seen in the company of a shoplifter, and 5 of 20 suspects against whom the only evidence was that they were found at or near the scene of a disturbance, made a confession or an admission. A number of persons suspected of other offences also made damaging statements where the existing evidence was somewhat weak. Nevertheless, the evidence against most suspects was highly incriminating, and an analysis of the outcome of interviews, in relation to the existing evidence, suggests that suspects were more likely to make a confession where the evidence against them was relatively strong. For example, among 9 persons suspected of burglary who were observed and detained at the scene of the crime, 7 made a confession, and, among 37 persons interviewed at the police station after they had been seen to take goods from a store and leave without paying, 28 (three quarters) made a confession. Such findings detract somewhat from the notion that interviews are always crucial for the detection of crime.

When they were asked what they would have done if the suspect had refused to answer questions, in 56 per cent of cases officers said that they would have relied on the evidence already available, in 32 per cent of cases they said that they would have tried to obtain additional evidence, and only in 8 per cent of cases did they say that they would have dropped the case.[1] In 12 of the 15 cases where the police said that they would have dropped the case, the suspect was actually released. If the police would have been prepared to rely on the existing evidence, why did they bother to question the suspect?

In the majority of cases, the purpose of questioning was, firstly, to decide whether there was sufficient evidence to prosecute and, secondly, to put together as strong a case as possible for the prosecution. When a suspect is taken into custody after an offence has been committed, the police still have a great deal of work to do in preparing a case for the court hearing. For this, questioning seems to be particularly valuable. When investigating officers were asked their opinion of the value of information given by the suspect during interview, in over 70 per cent of cases they said that it would help to secure a conviction if the case went to court. If questioning leads to a full confession, the police can hope for no more – though the confession may later be retracted in court. Although the police would have been prepared to prosecute most suspects on the basis of the evidence that was available prior to questioning, interviewing suspects could strengthen the case against them and possibly reduce the number of offenders who would escape conviction. Alternatively, it could, as discussed elsewhere in this report, help to establish suspects' innocence. Questioning could also provide useful information – either incriminatory or exculpatory – about co-suspects, or could provide potentially useful information about other persons. Forty three per cent of suspects questioned at the station provided information of this sort.

A further use of questioning was to provide a shortcut to the successful conclusion of an investigation and thereby save the police valuable time. In over 30 per cent of cases investigating officers said that, if the suspect had refused to answer their questions, they would have tried to obtain additional evidence. It is possible that, in some of these cases, the additional evidence – no matter how diligently it was sought – might not have been forthcoming.

So far, the discussion has focused on the suspect's part in the offence under investigation. If the impression has been given that the contribution of questioning to the detection of crime is a modest and somewhat pedestrian one, the explanation lies in the limited scope for the suspect to make novel and spectacular revelations. Just as it would be wrong for the police to arrest a person without reasonable grounds, so it would be unrealistic to expect that a suspect would make a confession if he were convinced that his guilt could not be proved. However, a number of suspects, having confessed to the offence under investigation, were persuaded to admit other offences. This did not happen very often – 17 per cent of suspects gave information about other offences – but, when it did happen, the results were often very impressive in

---

[1] In the remaining 4 per cent of cases in which the suspect was interviewed at the police station, all questions were refused.

terms of the number of crimes that were cleared up.[1] Indeed, for some suspects, offences which were not made the subject of charges but which were listed for consideration by the court determining sentence reached well into double figures. At times, therefore, questioning did lead to results which corresponded with the layman's view of the detection of crime: that is, it led either to the detection of unreported crimes or to the swift resolution of crimes that had been reported.

---

[1] Statistical returns made by police forces to the Home Office showed that, in 1977, approximately 25 per cent of crimes cleared up by the police were taken into consideration for sentencing purposes.

CHAPTER 7

The formal disposal of suspects

The final stage of the proceedings, observed by members of the research team at the police station, was the formal disposal of suspects on the occasion of their first appearance at the station in connection with the offence under investigation. The disposal on this occasion is shown in Table 7:1.

Table 7:1 Initial police disposal

Initial police disposal	Suspects	
	No.	%
Released unconditionally	24	11.0
Bailed 38(2) or told to come back to the station	49	22.4
Cautioned[1]	3	1.4
Reported for decision whether to prosecute	47	21.6
Charged	95	43.6
Total	*218*	*100.0*

Approximately one-tenth of suspects were released unconditionally; over one-fifth were bailed[2] under section 38(2) of the Magistrates' Courts Act of 1952, or were simply told to come back to the station; and nearly two-thirds were either charged or reported for a decision whether to prosecute. Of those who were charged, 66 were released on bail and 29 were detained after charging.

Table 7:2 analyses the relationship between the disposal of suspects and whether they had made a confession or an admission. The results show clearly that suspects who had confessed were more likely than others to be charged or reported for a decision whether to prosecute, and that suspects who had neither confessed nor made an admission were more likely to be released unconditionally or bailed to return to the station after the police had made further inquiries.

---

[1] 'Cautioned' in this chapter means the formal admonition given in place of prosecution.
[2] Forty-five suspects were formally bailed to return to the police station.

Table 7:2 Initial police disposal by whether the suspect made a confession or an admission

Initial police disposal	Whether the suspect had made a confession or an admission		
	Confession	Admission	Neither confession, nor admission
	Suspects %	Suspects %	Suspects %
Released	0.0	0.0	26.1
Bailed 38(2) or told to come back to the station	9.9	24.0	35.9
Cautioned	2.0	4.0	0.0
Reported for decision whether to prosecute	29.7	28.0	10.9
Charged	58.4	44.0	27.2
Total	*100.0*	*100.0*	*100.0*
	(N = 101[1])	(N = 25)	(N = 92)

[1] Of these, 89 confessed during an interview at the police station and 12, who were not interviewed, had admitted the offence before they were brought to the station.

The choice between charging a suspect or reporting him to senior officers was related to the suspect's record and the gravity of the offence. Among suspects who were either charged or reported, a fifth of those with a criminal record, compared with one half of those with no such record, were reported. None of the persons suspected of burglary was reported.

Of the 95 suspects charged at the police station, 67 were charged with one offence, 21 were charged on two counts and 7 on three. Just over a quarter (34) of the 130 charges were supported by a written confession or a written admission.

At the time of writing, proceedings had been concluded in respect of 168 of the 218 suspects. On the assumption that the remaining 50 suspects were prosecuted, Table 7:3 shows the final police disposal.[1]

Twenty two per cent of suspects (slightly over a fifth) were eventually released, 13 per cent were cautioned[2] and 65 per cent (almost two-thirds) were prosecuted. Almost one-half (21) of those who were released had been arrested in connection with a wounding or an assault. The relatively low prosecution rate for such offences is a reflection of the fact that multiple arrests were frequently made after a disturbance in a pub or the street, so that officers could determine who was responsible in the more sober atmosphere of the police station.

[1] As at least three, and in some instances six months had passed since these cases had been observed, it was assumed that if the police were going to release or caution these suspects they would have done so.

[2] Twenty four of the suspects who were cautioned were juveniles.

Table 7:3 Final police disposal

Final police disposal	Suspects	
	No.	%
Released	47	21.6
Cautioned	29	13.3
Prosecuted	142	65.1
Total	*218*	*100.0*

Of the 49 suspects who had initially been bailed or told to return to the police station, 21 were eventually released, 4 were cautioned and 24 (almost one half) were prosecuted. Of the 47 suspects who had been reported for a decision whether to prosecute, two were released, 22 were cautioned and 23 (almost one half) were prosecuted.

Almost four fifths of those who had made a confession were prosecuted and slightly more than a fifth were cautioned. Among those who had neither confessed nor made an admission, one half were released and one half were prosecuted. Fifty five per cent of those who were prosecuted had made a confession, 13 per cent had made an admission and 32 per cent had neither confessed nor made an admission.

Persons with a criminal record were not appreciably more likely than others to be released. However, they were more likely to be prosecuted and less likely to be cautioned than those with no criminal record. Almost four fifths (78 per cent) of those with a criminal record were prosecuted.

Full information about the result of court proceedings was available for only 91 suspects. Seventy seven pleaded guilty to all charges and 14 pleaded not guilty to at least one charge. Five of the latter were acquitted. Although these provisional figures are based on an incomplete and unrepresentative sample, it is worth noting that, not unexpectedly, suspects who had confessed were more likely than others to plead guilty. Only two among 57 suspects who had made a confession pleaded not guilty, whereas 12 of 34 suspects who had not made a confession pleaded not guilty. None of the five who were found not guilty had confessed during an interview at the police station: as a matter of fact, only one of the five had been interviewed.

Bearing in mind that the admissibility of statements alleged to have been made to the police is sometimes disputed, it is of particular interest that two of the suspects who had made a confession at the police station subsequently retracted the statement and pleaded not guilty. Both suspects had made written confessions in the presence of a member of the research team. One of them had made a written confession to assault occasioning actual bodily harm but had denied a more serious offence of wounding a second person. There was an independent witness to the second offence who made a statement incriminating the suspect. The suspect was charged with two offences and subsequently pleaded not guilty to both charges. He was found guilty of both offences.

The other suspect had made a written confession to two offences of burglary. He was charged with the two offences and subsequently pleaded not guilty to both charges. He was convicted on both counts.

In the opinion of observers (who did not attend the court hearings), the written confessions in these cases had been made voluntarily and accurately reflected previous accounts given by the suspects to the police.

CHAPTER 8

Summary and conclusions

The Judges' Rules and Administrative Directions to the Police and the treatment of persons in police custody have in recent years been the subject of a public debate, a clash of opinion between those who believe that the powers of the police to question suspects should be enlarged and those who believe that such powers should, in effect, be curbed. The tension manifested in the debate has two principal sources. First, questioning at the police station is not open to public scrutiny and, second, the rules that regulate such questioning have evolved from principles that can only uneasily be reconciled with present-day police practice.

Much of the criticism of police practice has been ill-informed, because police questioning is, understandably, conducted behind closed doors. Public knowledge and perceptions of police interrogation are largely based on 'causes célèbres', which are, by definition, exceptional cases, and on the accounts of prisoners.

The object of the study reported here was to provide an account, with reference to the general run of cases, of what happens to suspects from the time they arrive at the police station until they are released or put into a cell after being charged. To achieve this object, a team of observers from the Home Office Research Unit was allowed access to four police stations – one in the North, one in the Midlands, one in the West and one in London. During periods of attachment between 1 February and 1 May 1979, the team aimed at 24 hour coverage and attempted to follow through as many criminal cases as possible. The final sample consisted of 218 suspects.

The study had a number of limitations. The sample was not nationally representative although the four police stations involved were in major cities in different regions of England and the sample covered a wide range of criminal offences, if not exceptionally serious ones. The method of direct observation, given the limited time (slightly less than 1,000 hours) spent at the police stations and the sensitive nature of the practices under observation, is more likely to have yielded reliable information about routine or trivial breaches than exceptional or serious breaches of the Judges' Rules. Finally, the study does not purport to deal with the most serious criminal cases where the requirements of the Judges' Rules may impose a special strain on police officers; but it should be noted that it is not exclusively in relation to serious crimes that concern about observance of the Judges' Rules has been publicly expressed.

These limitations should all be borne in mind in reading this chapter, the purpose of which is to draw some tentative conclusions from the study. These relate to:

a. the value of questioning at the police station (i.e. post-arrest and pre-charge questioning);
b. adherence to the Judges' Rules, and
c. the appropriateness of those Rules.

The value of questioning at the police station

Nearly one half of the suspects who were interviewed at the police station made a confession and over two-thirds gave information which would help to secure a conviction. A substantial minority (almost a fifth of suspects) volunteered information about offences other than those for which they had been detained. It follows that, if the power of the police to question persons in their custody were curbed, the numbers of offenders who escape conviction would tend to increase and the detection rate would tend to fall. These effects would not necessarily be dramatic in terms of rates. In only 8 per cent of cases did the officers interviewed say that they would have dropped the case if the suspect had refused to answer questions, while in 56 per cent of cases they said that they would have relied on the evidence already available.

Adherence to the Judges' Rules

On balance, the police kept close to the spirit if not always to the letter of the Judges' Rules in the way they treated suspects. A few apparent breaches of the Rules and of the principles underlying these Rules occurred. For example, a few juveniles were not interviewed in the presence of a suitable adult; the police were occasionally slow to respond to a suspect's request to contact a solicitor; they sometimes omitted to caution suspects when they questioned them, and they may on occasion have given suspects more encouragement to make verbal or written confessions than the strict criteria of voluntariness allow.

The occurrence of technical infringements, even where an independent observer was present, may suggest that independent scrutiny of the questioning of suspects at the police station is desirable. On the other hand, the overall fairness of police practice, as assessed by observers, and the absence of any incident that was liable to impair the reliability of prosecution evidence may suggest that the police could be expected in the general run of cases to deal with suspects in accordance with realistic rules.

Information about the extent to which defendants retract statements made to the police is needed before a final decision can be made on the merits of some form of independent scrutiny of the questioning of suspects. The incomplete results of the present study showed that, among 91 suspects who were prosecuted, 77 pleaded guilty to all charges and 14 pleaded not guilty to at least one charge. Two of those who pleaded not guilty apparently retracted a confession: both of them were convicted.

94

One further point on the merits of some form of independent scrutiny should be considered. Any measures which reduce the number of suspects who confess could increase the number of defendants who plead not guilty.

The appropriateness of the Judges' Rules

Apart from the matter of adherence to the Rules, there is the question of the appropriateness of the Rules. There is arguably a contradiction in the present Rules between the entitlement of police officers to question a suspect who has been taken into custody, which is conferred by Rule 1, and the right of a suspect to remain silent, which is sanctioned by the requirement in Rule II that a person shall be cautioned as soon as a police officer has evidence which would afford reasonable grounds for suspecting that he has committed an offence. The proper nature of post-arrest questioning and the period for which a suspect may be held for questioning prior to charging are not dealt with by the Judges' Rules, though principle (e) in the introduction to the present Rules stipulates that it is a fundamental condition of the admissibility in evidence of a statement by a suspect that it shall have been voluntary, and section 38 of the Magistrates' Courts Act 1952, as amended by the Bail Act 1976, stipulates that a person taken into custody for an offence without a warrant shall be brought before a magistrates' court or bailed within 24 hours, unless the offence appears to the officer in charge of the station to be a serious one. It seemed to observers that some reliable confessions were made which did not flow freely from a strong sense of guilt. Confessions may be made for a variety of reasons and it needs to be stated frankly that, in the opinion of observers, they were often made because they were an easy and logical way out of a tense and uncomfortable situation created by persistent and determined police officers. In relation, for example, to the taking of a written statement under caution, the present Rules convey an image of a suspect announcing to an astonished and suitably silent police officer, waiting patiently by his side: 'I wish to make a statement!' If more weight is to be given to the principle of voluntariness and the right of suspects to remain silent, it may be necessary to reduce the freedom of the police to question suspects. But, if the practice of questioning suspects in custody is to be sanctioned, then it may be considered that the criteria of voluntariness are unrealistically strict and could be more readily adhered to if they were relaxed. Furthermore, if police officers are entitled to question suspects, then it would be logical to expect that suspects should have a corresponding obligation to answer their questions or risk having adverse inferences drawn against them at their trial. Such a restriction of the right to silence could reduce the need for police officers to encourage suspects to talk and would help to relieve officers' anxiety that the presence of a solicitor at the police station would impede their enquiries.

In advocating a restriction of the right to silence, the Criminal Law Revision Committee and Sir Robert Mark (1973) have argued that there is an increasing class of sophisticated criminals who are well aware of their legal rights and use every possible means to avoid conviction. The authors of a recently published study of jury trials[1] express the opinion that the Committee's proposal to dismantle the right to silence was undermined because of the lack of any empirical support for this contention.[2] The present study includes few criminals whom the police would regard as sophisticated and was not designed to ascertain whether the number of sophisticated criminals is increasing, but it has shown that suspects with a criminal record were more likely than others to ask to see a solicitor at the police station and to exercise their right to silence, and were less likely than others to make a confession or an admission.

Whatever decisions are taken about the proper balance between the powers of the police and the rights of people suspected of crime, it seems clear that the effects will not be confined to the police station. Policemen and lawyers, the main protagonists in the current debate, are spokesmen not only for their professions but also for the general public who as potential victims or suspects have an unquestionable stake in the outcome.

---

[1] Baldwin and McConville (1979) p.106

[2] It has been established by Zander (1974) that, in the Crown Court, the defendant with a prior record has a lower rather than a higher chance of acquittal than someone with no previous convictions.

References

Baldwin, J. and McConville, M. 1979 *Jury Trials.* Clarendon Press, Oxford.

Criminal Law Revision Committee 1972 *Eleventh Report: Evidence (General).* Cmnd. 4991. HMSO, London.

Home Office 1978 *Judges' Rules and Administrative Directions to the Police.* Circular No. 89/1978. HMSO, London.

Mark, R. 1973 *Minority Verdict.* The 1973 Dimbleby Lecture. BBC Publications, London.

Wald, M., Ayres, R., Hess, D.W., Schantz, M. and Whitebread, C.H. 1967 Interrogations in New Haven: the impact of *Miranda. Yale Law Journal,* 76, 1519-1648.

Zander, M. 1974 Are too many professional criminals avoiding conviction? A study of Britain's two busiest courts. *Mod. Law Rev.,* 37, 28-61.

Nature of evidence against suspects for selected categories of crime

Table A:1 Nature of the information against persons suspected of burglary

Nature of information	Suspects	
	No.	%
Observed and detained at scene of crime	9	39.1
Observed at scene of crime and detained nearby shortly after offence had been committed	4	17.4
Identified by forensic or other physical evidence found at scene of crime	3	13.0
Suspected as having been at scene of crime, but not identified by physical evidence or witness other than prisoner or informer	7	30.4
Total	*23*	*100.0*

Table A:2 Nature of the information against persons suspected of theft from a store

Nature of information	Suspects	
	No.	%
Seen to take goods and leave store without paying	47	71.2
Seen to take goods and leave department (but not store premises) without paying	7	10.6
Not seen to take goods, but seen to leave store without paying for goods found in suspect's possession	3	4.5
Seen in company of shoplifter	9	13.6
Total	*66*	*100.0*

Table A:3 Nature of the information against persons suspected of other theft

Nature of information	Suspects	
	No.	%
Caught in the act	3	9.4
Found in possession of property that was stolen or believed to be stolen	20	62.5
Seen in company of persons suspected of theft, but not found in possession of incriminating evidence prior to arrest	6	18.7
Suspected on the basis of opportunity/known whereabouts, but not found in possession of incriminating evidence prior to arrest	2	6.3
No information[1]	1	3.1
Total	*32*	*100.0*

Table A:4 Nature of the information against persons suspected of wounding or assault

Nature of information	Suspects	
	No.	%
Identified as culprit	22	50.0
Found at or near scene of disturbance/identified as having been at scene of disturbance	21	47.7
No information[1]	1	2.3
Total	*44*	*100.0*

Table A:5 Nature of the information against persons suspected of other offences

Nature of information	Suspects	
	No.	%
Caught in the act/seen committing offence	26	49.0
Incriminating evidence found in suspect's possession	9	17.0
Observed at or near scene of crime or in the company of suspects	17	32.1
No information[1]	1	1.9
Total	*53*	*100.0*

[1] In Tables A:3 to A:5, 'No information' refers to the fact that the only evidence was initially the suspect's own admission.